This book is dedicated to

Jay Adams

A true hero of the faith in the biblical counseling movement.
I consider it a privilege to have known him and learned so much from him.

Acknowledgments

I wrote this book while I was on COVID-19 lockdown. The first day of the lockdown, I cleaned out our pantry. That took a half a day. You should see it. It's wonderful. Then, I didn't know what to do after that. So I decided to write a book about biblical counseling. Thus, here it is.

I am so very grateful to the Lord for all the help He gives me. As with almost all of my previous books, my pastor, John Crotts, and my daughter, Anna Maupin, did the lion's share of the editing. John corrects any Scriptures that are out of context and Anna checks my sentence structure. Both have insightful and helpful suggestions.

Jan Haley, owner of Focus Publishing, greatly helped me to be clearer in areas where I was vague or fuzzy. We had fun working through this manuscript together.

Last, but not least, are my two good friends – Christie Hopkins and Jenny Aspacher. The three of us discovered that if we read the book aloud, we would find more corrections to be made. So, we met together once a week and took turns reading one or two chapters aloud. I told them they are my "personal assistants." They were a tremendous blessing to me.

God gave me a forced "time on my hands" *and* the desire to write this book. I am praying that He will use it for His glory and for it to be a practical help for biblical counselors as well as individuals who are struggling with the issues covered in this volume.

Table of Contents

Introduction

1. Counseling Denise: An Amazing Story of the Power of God 1

2. Counseling Helps to Safely Come off Antidepressants 17

3. Counseling Women to Have a Gentle and Quiet Spirit 27

4. Counseling Women Who are Deeply Emotionally Disturbed 51

5. Counseling Women in Abusive Relationships 63

6. Counseling and Correcting Wrong Ways to
   Think About Biblical Submission 75

7. Counseling Women Who Desire to be Equal 89

8. Counseling Women Who are Depressed 97

9. Counseling Women Who are Anxious 107

10. Counseling Women to be Godly Mothers 119

11. Counseling Women Going Through a Divorce 135

12. Counseling Women Who Struggle with Pornography 147

Introduction

I have been certified as a biblical counselor working with women for over thirty years. It has been the ministry that the Lord has given me even though, at times, I would have preferred to be doing something else. My church, Faith Bible Church in Sharpsburg, Georgia, is an official Biblical Counseling Training Center through the Association of Certified Biblical Counselors (biblicalcounseling.com).

Before I was a Christian, I worked for thirteen years as a nurse in a pediatric intensive care unit in a large hospital in Atlanta, Georgia, and taught critical care nursing at Clayton State College near Atlanta. It was during my years at Clayton State that the Lord saved me and totally changed the direction of my life. I was halfway through my master's degree in nursing at a large university in Atlanta when the Lord convicted me that I needed to be home with my family. I wrote a letter to the Dean of the nursing department of the university and said, "I have become a Christian and the Lord Jesus is coming back. I don't have time for this, so withdraw me from the program." Well, they certainly did! Two years later, I resigned from my teaching job and have never regretted it. Providentially, God has used my nurse's training to be especially helpful while counseling biblically.

For years now, I have been a volunteer counselor, working with a team of certified counselors from our church headed up by David Birch, one of our pastors. Over time, I have counseled and observed many difficult women's problems. I have also researched, written about, and lectured on different issues. This book presents a variety of different counseling issues with biblical counseling practical tips for helping those who struggle.

Each chapter stands by itself and there is a great variety of topics. It is my prayer that God will use this material to enable many counselors and lay persons to help Christians turn from their struggles and go to Him in repentance and faith. David, the Shepherd boy in Israel who grew up to become their king, said it best:

Psalm 19:7-11
A Psalm of David

The law of the LORD is perfect, restoring the soul;

The testimony of the LORD is sure, making wise the simple.

The precepts of the LORD are right, rejoicing the heart;

The commandment of the LORD is pure, enlightening the eyes.

The fear of the LORD is clean, enduring forever;

The judgments of the LORD are true; they are righteous altogether.

They are more desirable than gold, yes, than much fine gold;

Sweeter also than honey and the drippings of the honeycomb.

Moreover, by them Your servant is warned;

In keeping them there is great reward…

Chapter One

Counseling Denise
An Amazing Story of the Power of God
(Shared with Permission of Denise)

One Thursday morning in May a few years ago, I arrived at church for my day of volunteer counseling. I knew I was scheduled to see back-to-back counselees all day long. When I arrived, Rita, the church administrative assistant, told me she had received a call from a mother whose fifteen-year-old daughter would not eat, drink anything, or talk. Her parents were at their wits end and had heard about me, so the mother asked if she could come with her daughter to see me that day?

I asked Rita to call them back and tell them to come at my lunch break, but the girl's father had to come also. I wanted to not only see this gal but also both of her parents together. They were to come early and fill out the data information forms.

I was startled when I saw Denise for the first time. She was frail, weak, and starving herself. Her parents had to help her walk and guide her to the chair. At home, her mom had to take her to the bathroom and bathe her. Denise would not look at me or talk to me. There was no expression on her face. She was in a catatonic state, and the only reason her parents could come up with was that she was worried about her salvation. It seemed to me that there was more to the story than that. Something was terribly wrong, and whatever it was, it was disturbing and imminently life threatening.

Talking with Denise's parents with her sitting there with us, I learned that she was fifteen years old and was home-schooled. Advanced for her age in school, she was a hard worker and very smart. She was artistic and could draw beautifully. The family had ten children and she was number eight out of ten. Her parents described her as quiet, compliant, and a perfectionist.

In getting to know her parents, I found out they were Bible believing Christians and regularly active in their church. One thing they were adamant about is that they were very distrustful of receiving help from the psychiatric/psychologic route.

Counseling Papers Filled Out
The Beginning of Data Gathering

Denise's mom filled out the application for counseling forms and stated that Denise's main goal was to "recover from anorexia and work through other conflicts immobilizing her life." In answer to the question, "What have you done to try and resolve the problem?" she wrote, "Prayed, fasted, gone over Scripture, and tried to reason with Denise." The issues she wanted resolved were "eating, schoolwork, withdrawing, uncertainty in deciding what is right, and what is God's will." The next question was "What do you want us to do?" The answer was, "to resolve the previous question, or at least make progress to restore a normal function level."

Denise's mom saw her "up until the recent crisis as capable, taking initiative, loving, giving, kind, and excelling in all she does, wanting to please God and obey the Scriptures." In reply to "Is there any other information we should know?" her mom wrote, "She seems immobilized by fear of being wrong, and because of her indecision, seems to believe there is some question on which all this is based which she must decide but is not sure God wants her to tell it." I questioned the parents about her physical health, and they had already taken her to her pediatrician for a complete physical. Everything was normal except, of course, her weight.

Looking back on her counseling, I have divided the time into phases based on medical categories that show her progress.

Phase One of Counseling
Gravely Ill

Of course, I was hesitant to take on such a serious counselee and would not have except that her parents were so committed to the Lord, but I

Counseling Denise: An Amazing Story of the Power of God

gave them several stipulations. I believe the Lord gave me a heart to try to help. The first few weeks, I met with Denise and her mom three times a week and was in touch with her mom on the days we did not meet.

I remembered something that I heard Jay Adams teach—that if you have someone catatonic who will not communicate with you, talk to them as if they are understanding and comprehending. In other words, talk to the counselee by faith and not by sight. So, I prayed and prayed and prayed and that is what I did.

I could not tell if Denise was hearing me or if she was listening to me. I knew that even if she could hear me, she was not getting enough nutrients to her brain to think straight. The brain functions on carbohydrates and she was not eating anything. Her parents' best guess was that she was fearful about her salvation, but it just seemed there had to be more.

Even though I was very disturbed by how Denise looked and was acting, I pretended like this was routine and, at least, outwardly stayed calm and matter of fact. Session after session, I began with asking Denise questions and told her she had to answer me.

> "Denise, what has happened?"
>
> "Why are you so upset and are afraid to tell us?"
>
> "Has someone hurt you in any way?"
>
> "What's wrong?"
>
> "Were you sexually molested?"

Time after time, there was no answer and no indication that she comprehended what I was asking. Her mom took detailed notes throughout each session. Denise's mom was to be her advocate and to come each session. She was to take notes and go over them with Denise in-between sessions. I also gave them a list of simple "emergency thoughts" that were intended to give Denise, her mom, and myself hope. She could read those emergency thoughts aloud to

Denise especially before meals.

These are the thoughts:

> "I *am* going to eat even though I am scared."

> "Thank You Lord for this food" (1 Thessalonians 5:18).

> "Help me to take the first bite."

> **"I sought the Lord, and He answered me, and delivered me from all of my fears"** (Psalms 34:4).

Then I followed up with detailed medical instructions. The first was that they must have an appointment with a board-certified psychiatrist, or I would not counsel her. They would also have to give me and the doctor permission to consult with each other. This was difficult for the parents, but they agreed when I told them that there might be a suggestion from the doctor or even a medication that could, at least, temporarily help her to begin communicating with us.

I told them to take Denise to the emergency room at the hospital if she gets weak, dehydrated, or about to faint. It was better to be safe than sorry. I cautioned them that the emergency room personnel will be suspicious of them and report them to Family and Children's Services if they did not already have an appointment with a psychiatrist. It was only a day or two later that they did have to take her to the emergency room because she became so dehydrated. The doctor gave her fluids and allowed them to go home because of the scheduled psychiatric appointment. Denise would not communicate with the doctor either, but after this experience she began to eat and drink a small amount.

In addition, I required written permission for me to talk with Denise's pediatrician. So, her mom agreed to give him permission to talk with me. During those first few weeks, I did talk with her pediatrician once (as we were still waiting on the psychiatric appointment) and asked him if he would consider giving her a very mild tranquilizer for a short term. My thinking was it possibly could relax her enough to then tell us what was wrong. He was not comfortable doing that, so he said, "no."

Counseling Denise: An Amazing Story of the Power of God

The first few weeks were difficult and scary. For the first time in thirty years of counseling, I left in the middle of the session and burst into tears. I went to my assistant Rita and asked her to send out an e-mail to our entire church family, asking them to pray for a counselee I had and tell them that I was frightened and wondered if she would live.

Summer had arrived and the weather was nice. As a result, I began walking in our neighborhood each morning and praying. I begged God for wisdom and asked Him to give Denise a sound mind.

Early in the process, I bought Denise a present. It was a beautiful journal for her to write in. I wrapped it up and gave it to her. She would not even look at it or touch it, so her mom opened it for her. I told her this is a "Think These Thoughts" journal. My instruction was that only good thoughts and helpful Scriptures were to be written in it. The first thing I asked Mom to write in it was, **"Trust in the LORD with all your heart and do not lean on your own understanding"** (Proverbs 3:5).

I clung to the absolute belief that **"faith comes by hearing,"** and we were giving Denise truth (Romans 10:17). I truly did believe that God would give me wisdom and that you cannot get any deeper inside a person than the **"thoughts and intentions of the heart"** and that is what the Scriptures do (Hebrews 4:12). It also encouraged me that her family was exceptionally encouraging throughout. So, I began teaching Denise basic doctrine and, by faith, hoped it was sinking in or at least scratching the surface.

During that gravely ill time, I gave Denise homework. It was actually her mom doing the homework for her. There were five assignments:

1. Eat at least 1,000 calories per day.
2. Keep a food diary with calorie count.
3. Keep a self-talk log in which you write down what you are thinking when you have emotional pain.
4. Daily Bible reading in the Gospel of John.
5. Daily prayers.

This went on for a few weeks with us meeting three times a week. She was still not talking.

**Phase Two of Counseling
Critical**

This phase lasted several weeks but there were little glimmers of hope. She had begun eating a little since the ER visit. She obeyed her dad by eating when he was there, so I instructed her mom to get Denise up to eat breakfast each day with her dad. As it turned out, breakfast became her best meal, and she would eat it rapidly so she could go back to bed.

With all her meals, if Denise would be hesitant to eat, her mom would read out loud the "Think These Thoughts" journal entries and then the family would go ahead and eat. Each time I saw Denise in a counseling session, I would go over the same questions but get no response. One day, in jest, I added the question, "Are you doing cocaine?" She did not answer me but obviously she thought that was funny because a little smile appeared on her face and quickly disappeared. That was all I needed to know that she comprehended what I was saying.

In another session, when she did not answer me, I said, "Denise, it is rude when you don't talk to me and answer my questions." I told Denise that **"Love ... does not act unbecomingly"** (1 Corinthians 13: 5). Both her mom and I look back on that time as a major turning point, but Denise was still bound up in her catatonic state.

I have found it helpful when someone is psychotic or delusional to tell them the truth simply and quietly. Each session, I would ask questions and teach her some foundational truth such as the Gospel, the doctrine of sanctification, and the put-off and put-on teaching in the Scriptures. Basically, I went over Bible studies that I had written and are free downloads on my blog site: marthapeacetew@blogspot.com.

I began with the Gospel and over the first weeks of counseling, I explained the Gospel several different times using a variety of Scriptures. I started with the following:

1. God is holy and is untouched by even a shadow of sin.

> **In the year of King Uzziah's death I [Isaiah] saw the Lord sitting on a throne, lofty and exalted, with the train of His robe filing the temple. Seraphim**

> [one kind of angel] **stood above Him, each having six wings: with two he covered his face, and with two he covered his feet, and with two he flew. And one called out to another and said, "Holy, Holy, Holy, is the LORD of hosts** [the angel armies], **the whole earth is full of His glory." And the foundations of the thresholds trembled at the voice of him who called out, while the temple was filling with smoke. Then I said, "Woe is me, for I am ruined! Because I am a man of unclean lips, and I live among a people of unclean lips; For my eyes have seen the King the LORD of hosts."** [Isaiah saw his sin in a way he had never seen it before, and he was devastated!] (Isaiah 6:1-5, explanation mine.)

2. We are not holy. We are sinners and deserve to die and be punished for our sin. God is our perfect Creator and we are His creatures, therefore we are obligated to obey Him perfectly.

> **… for all have sinned and fall short of the glory of God** (Romans 3:23).

> **And you were dead in your trespasses and sins, in which you formerly walked according to the course of this world…** (Ephesians 2:1-2).

3. You cannot ever do enough good works or be deserving enough to work your way into heaven. It is hopeless to even try because God's standard is to love Him and others perfectly. You cannot obtain salvation on your own.

> **But when the kindness of God our Savior and His love for mankind appeared, He saved us, not on the basis of deeds which we have done in righteousness, but according to His mercy, by the washing of regeneration and renewing by the Holy Spirit, whom He poured out upon us richly through Jesus Christ our Savior, so that being justified by His grace we would be made heirs according to the hope of eternal life** (Titus 3:4-7).

4. It is God's mercy, God's grace, and God's gift that makes it possible for us to be saved. God Himself in the form of a man, the Lord Jesus Christ, came to earth, was born of a virgin, lived a perfect life, and died an innocent man. He suffered incomprehensible agony on the cross as He took upon Himself the punishment that we deserve.

> **He** [God the Father] **made Him** [God the Son] **who knew no sin to be sin on our behalf, so that we might become the righteousness of God in Him** (2 Corinthians 5:21, explanation mine).

5. Christ's resurrection from the dead was the proof positive that He had done what He said He would do and that all who would believe would be saved.

> **He who was delivered over because of our transgressions, and was raised because of our justification** (Romans 4:25).
>
> **… that if you confess with your mouth Jesus as Lord, and believe in your heart that God raised Him from the dead, you will be saved** (Romans 10:9).
>
> **… for whoever will call on the name of the Lord will be saved** (Romans 10:13).
>
> **They said, "Believe in the Lord Jesus, and you will be saved, you and your household"** (Acts 16:31).

After the Gospel, I moved on to the doctrine of sanctification. The root word for sanctification in the Scriptures is *hagios* which means to be holy. God wants us to live holy lives. I explained to Denise that the Bible teaches three aspects of our holiness. The first is *positional* holiness. This aspect is a 100% work of God and it happens at the moment He saves you. The Holy Spirit draws you, convicts you of sin, grants you repentance and faith, cleanses you of your sin, and gives you a new heart. Peter is writing to Christians scattered throughout the Roman provinces, and he reminds them they were saved **"by the sanctifying work of the Spirit"** (1 Peter 1:2).

Counseling Denise: An Amazing Story of the Power of God

When Paul gave his testimony before King Agrippa, he explained that Jesus told him He was sending Paul to witness to the Gentiles. The purpose was **"...to open their eyes so that they may turn from darkness to light and from the dominion of Satan to God, that they may receive forgiveness of sins and an inheritance among those who have been sanctified by faith in Me"** (Acts 26:18).

The second aspect of sanctification is *progressive*. This is a lifelong process of being transformed into more of Christ's image. This begins at the moment of salvation and lasts until God takes you home to be with Him. This is being "in Christ" (think in union with Christ). This is a work of God convicting and empowering you to make you more like Jesus. However, it is not only a work of God, but it also is a work of man. In other words, you have a responsibility to **"discipline yourself for the purpose of godliness"** (1 Timothy 4:7).

Whatever happens to us is not by luck or fate. It is the providence of God. Paul tells us in Romans that even the difficult circumstances in our lives are for our good and for God's glory. Our "good" is Him making us more like Christ.

> **And we know that God causes all things to work together for good to those who love God** [those who are Christians], **to those who are called according to His purpose** [for His glory]. **For those whom He foreknew, He also predestined to become conformed to the image of His Son...** (Romans 8:28-29, explanation mind).

Paul writes about this glorious, supernatural transformation in 2 Corinthians 3:17-18:

> **Now the Lord is the Spirit, and where the Spirit of the Lord is, there is liberty. But we all, with unveiled face, beholding as in a mirror the glory of the Lord, are being transformed into the same image from glory to glory, just as from the Lord, the Spirit.**

The third and final aspect of sanctification is *perfection*. This, like the first aspect, is a 100% work of God and will happen when He takes us to be with Him in heaven. We will never sin again, and when Jesus comes back, we will be given our glorified bodies.

> **So also is the resurrection of the dead. It is sown a perishable body, it is raised an imperishable body; it is sown in dishonor, it is raised in glory; it is sown in weakness, it is raised in power, it is sown a natural body, it is raised a spiritual body...** (1 Corinthians 15:42-44).

Keep in mind that Denise was still not looking at me or talking to me or anyone else for that matter. But session after session, I kept teaching her. The next doctrine I taught her was the put-off and put-on concept in Ephesians.

> **... in reference to your former manner of life** [before you were saved], **you lay aside the old self, which is being corrupted in accordance with the lusts of deceit, and that you be renewed in the spirit of your mind, and put on the new self, which in the likeness of God has been created in righteousness and holiness of the truth** (Ephesians 4:22-24, explanation mine).

I gave her several examples of the put-off and put-on process and told her about renewing her mind. One example is, that instead of being angry and bitter, she should think kind and forgiving thoughts. Then I would just make up thoughts that I presumed she might possibly be thinking. Obviously, I was grasping at straws because I was still in the dark about what was in her heart (what she *was* thinking), but the Lord helped me to persevere by faith. It was certainly not by sight!

Next came the anxiety journal based on Philippians 4:6-9. I made up an example of a thought that she *might* be thinking and explained to her that each journal entry has three parts: a biblical prayer, a biblical thought, and biblical actions. Each thought is on one page of her journal and would look something like the following:

"I cannot take it anymore!"

Counseling Denise: An Amazing Story of the Power of God

1. **Biblical prayer** based on Philippians 4:6-7. The prayer has basically two parts: a request and thankfulness to God. A supplication is a humble request.

> **Be anxious for nothing, but in everything by prayer and supplication with thanksgiving let your requests be made known to God. And the peace of God, which surpasses all comprehension, will guard your hearts and your minds in Christ Jesus** (Philippians 4:6-7).

> Father,
> *My request is* that You will help me to cope with my circumstances. *Thank You* for reminding me how much I need You.
> In Jesus Name, Amen

2. **Biblical thought** based on Philippians 4:8. This is correcting the wrong thought and replacing it with a thought based on the criteria in Philippians 4:8:

> **Finally, brethren, whatever is true, whatever is honorable, whatever is right, whatever is pure, whatever is lovely, whatever is of good repute, if there is any excellence and if anything worthy of praise, dwell on these things.**

> Often, the thought would need to be corrected to become true and God-honoring such as honorable (God-honoring) and excellent and praiseworthy (pointing to God): "This is very difficult for me, but God will give me the grace to bear up under it." (Based on 1 Corinthians 10:13)

3. **Biblical actions** based on Philippians 4:9:

> **The things you have learned and received and heard and seen in me, practice these things, and the God of peace will be with you.**

Actions would be a list of things she could do to honor God and show love to others. Examples would be to complete her counseling homework, eat all her meals, and tell us the truth about what she is thinking.

At the end of each session, I would go over the emergency thoughts with her and add Scriptures and God-honoring thoughts to her journal. Homework during that period was (1) Go over the "Think These Thoughts" journal several times a day, (2) Add to the journal Hebrews 4:14-16; Matthew 11:29-31; Lamentations 3:21-25; 1 Corinthians 10:13, (3) Pray daily and ask God to help you. (4) Continue to eat the food Mom prepares for you.

Phase Three of Counseling
Critical but Stabilizing

One day at the beginning of our counseling session, I began to ask the same questions as always, and Denise began to answer me. I asked, "Denise, you have to tell me what has happened." She very hesitantly replied, "It's not what you think it is." I replied, "So, what is it?" She said, "God told me to not tell anyone until I got the issue of my salvation settled. He also told me that I could not eat or drink until it was settled." When she said that you could have knocked me over with a feather! Recovering, I replied something like, "God did not tell you that. He gives good things to believers and unbelievers alike. He *is* telling you through His Word, **"If you seek Me, you will find Me"** (Adapted from Proverbs 8:17).

Because of her twisted thinking about God, I started her on Arthur Pink's book, *The Attributes of God*. At the beginning, her mom had to read it to her. My instructions to them were to have a dictionary handy to look up any words that you do not know the meaning of, and when you come to a Scripture whether quoted or cited, stop, and look it up in your Bible. The chapters are short in Pink's book but full of amazing truth about God. He had a very biblical and high view of God.

We only completed one chapter per session, and we studied it paragraph by paragraph. I wanted her to tell me what stood out to her, and then I would tell her what stood out to me in a particular paragraph. Looking

Counseling Denise: An Amazing Story of the Power of God

back on those sessions, I think that God saved Denise about halfway through Arthur Pink's book. During those weeks, I cut down our counseling to twice a week. She was still struggling to eat normally, but that too was improving.

Phase Four of Counseling
Fair and Improving

I knew that Amy Baker, an ACBC counselor at Faith Church in Lafayette, Indiana, had completed a book on perfectionism entitled *Picture Perfect*. So even though the book was not yet published, I contacted Amy and told her about Denise. I asked her if she would be willing to send me the manuscript. Amy graciously shared her book with me. I printed out two copies, one for me and one for Denise.

Denise progressed to the place where she was willing to read by herself, so I instructed her to read several pages (not very many, I was specific), underline or highlight what she thought was important or what she had questions about. We went page by page with both of us sharing what we thought was important or convicting or what she had questions about.

During that fall, there were some backwards steps, especially concerning her legalistic rules. She decided that she could not go to the grocery store because the grocery stores require people to work on Sundays. Her thinking was that if you shop at a grocery store even during the week, you are making people sin. Another misguided belief was that she could not wear anything that had color in it because color was not modest. Then she decided to not use shampoo to wash her hair because it was an unnecessary expense. Instead, she used bar soap until her mom noticed that there was something wrong with her hair and asked her about it. At one point, I told Denise that she was the most creative legalist I had ever met! She was desperately trying to come up with a formula that worked for her to prove she was saved.

An interesting side note, because of the amazing, convoluted ways she connected the dots in her mind with Scriptures, I was almost tempted to tell her she could not read her Bible! I shared that thought privately with her mom and she told me that she had had the same thought. But, in the end, neither one of us told Denise she could not read her Bible.

During that time, I taught Denise about asceticism (extreme self-denial for religious reasons). Paul preaches against this thinking in Colossians, chapter two. People that struggle with asceticism believe that the more you suffer, the more holy you are. I also took her through Stuart Scott's book, *From Pride to Humility*, and the chapter on legalism from my book, *Damsels in Distress*.

Homework

1. Salvation Work Sheets by Martha Peace.
2. Put-Off and Put-On Bible study by Martha Peace.
3. I assigned Denise to include one page for each fear-producing thought she had in her anxiety journal. For example, "God told me that I may not eat until I know if I am saved."
4. Increased her calorie intake by telling her she had to eat all the food that was placed before her. I cautioned her mom to not overdo the portions.
5. Self-Talk Log: write down your thoughts when you feel anxious.
6. *Attitudes of a Transformed Heart* by Martha Peace: read chapter nine on how to think biblically and chapter thirteen on the heart's attitude of love.
7. *Attributes of God* by Arthur Pink.
8. *Damsels in Distress* by Martha Peace: read chapter eight on legalism. "I Just Love Rules, Don't You?"

Counseling Phase Five
Good and Mostly Praising the Lord

We began counseling on May 9 and finished Amy's book, *Picture Perfect*, on December 18, and Denise was dismissed from counseling. My "record" of that day states, "Denise is doing well. States she has some anxiety about salvation, but she is OK." Months later, I saw her mom and Denise at a conference where I was speaking, it was pure joy to see her rushing up to me with a smile on her face and to listen to her tell me all that she was doing. She was taking college classes and continuing to walk with the Lord in freedom.

Conclusion

Denise's issues at first frightened me and, at times, overwhelmed me. As I would remind her that she could **"not lean on her own understanding,"** I was talking to myself also, (Proverbs 5:3). I heeded Jay Adams' advice and talked to her and taught her about God. I prayed she was listening, and that God would enlighten her mind to understand. Those first few weeks were confusing, and every day I was begging God for wisdom. I taught her basic Bible doctrine and prayed for wisdom and that Denise would comprehend what I was telling her. In the end, God's mercy, awesome power, and love was clear to see.

Much later, I phoned her mom and we talked about what had happened. She believes that Denise was desperately trying to figure out a formula from the Old Testament and New Testament that would work to please God and assure her of her salvation. I believe that God was testing *my* faith and showing *me* His awesome goodness and power.

Biblical Counseling in Practice

Chapter Two

Counseling Helps to Safely Come Off Antidepressants

Special thanks to Dr. Laura Hendrickson, MD and Board-Certified Psychiatrist for her help and insights and Dr. Charles Hodges, MD for his insights.

When I became a biblical counselor over thirty years ago, antidepressant medication was not common. However, over the years I have seen it become a huge issue with some counselees being on several antidepressants, and even antipsychotic medications at the same time. Most of my counselees do not like the side effects and have a desire to come off the drug(s). They express that desire usually at the first session, and I have not even mentioned the topic.

What I tell them is, "Let's just wait for a while and then when you and I think you are ready to come off of one or more medications, I will give you some tips on what to tell your doctor. He will have to prescribe the lower doses."

But before we get to the "tips," let me give you a very brief history of psychiatric drugs.

Psychiatric Drugs Come and Go

It has always been a challenge to try and control the behavior of someone who is acting in bizarre ways. More than one hundred years ago the psychiatric drug "of the day" was cocaine. Obviously, cocaine would perk a depressed patient up very quickly, but it had the unfortunate side effect of being highly addictive. Sometimes with just one dose!

Not long before I was in nursing school in the mid-1960's, psychiatrists experimented with giving violent or depressed patients insulin to place them in insulin shock. The patients' blood sugar would plummet, and it would cause damage to brain cells. The thought behind it was that the patient would not remember why they were so depressed. Since the brain requires carbohydrates (sugars) to function, the theory was it would be worth killing some brain cells if, afterwards, the patient would perk up. Well, that theory did not last very long as it was so dangerous to the patient's life and well-being.

In the 1960's, the main treatments for psychiatric problems were Thorazine, Librium, phenobarbital, and shock treatments. Shock treatments were popular back then and are still used today but to a much lesser degree. The shock treatments cause a patient to have a short-term memory loss and the hope is that they will not remember why they were so upset and depressed. Like insulin shock therapy, shock treatments cause some death of brain cells. As a student nurse in psychiatric nursing, I remember assisting the doctor carrying out the shock treatments. The patient was sedated and did not feel pain, but it was a difficult procedure for me to observe.

Over the past seventy years, the psychiatric drugs have come and gone. There is a pattern that has emerged: at first the drug is touted by the drug company as safe and non-addictive. Time has told otherwise. Since 1987 when Prozac came out, we have seen the emergence of the anti-depressants. It has never been established *how* these drugs lift someone's mood. However, for some people they *will* do that at least for a while.

These drugs are chemically related to methamphetamines. The drug companies started developing anti-depressants with the chemical makeup of meth. They tweaked it until they developed a safer version with fewer side-effects. The theory of the medical community was that depression is caused by a chemical imbalance in the brain.

In the brain there are neurotransmitters (dopamine, serotonin, and norepinephrine) in the fluid spaces (cerebral-spinal fluid) that facilitate neurological signals to race through the brain for the body to function as it should. Interestingly, the multitude of microscopic brain cells composes these chemicals from within the cell themselves. When there is not enough neurotransmitter in the fluid spaces, just the right amount of "chemical" moves through the semi-permeable wall of the tiny little cell and into the fluid space. The chemicals shift back and forth from fluid space to cell to balance them out perfectly. You must be in awe of the miracle of God's creation.

Counseling Helps to Safely Come Off Antidepressants

So, because methamphetamines and now anti-depressants are known to dramatically increase the neurotransmitter levels in the fluid spaces, and they do perk up the patient, it was theorized that depression was caused by an imbalance. So, the drug companies have continued to make Prozac-like drugs. The problem is that the chemical imbalance theory is not true. It reminds me of the theory of evolution. Scientists know it is only a *theory* and not proven, but they believe it anyway. Psychiatrists would tell patients who were depressed that they had a disease due to a chemical imbalance in their brain that caused their depression. So, they had to have the medicine to balance it out. However, some preeminent psychiatrists were questioning and writing very early that the theory was not true. Now all psychiatrists are saying that. My counselees would tell me they had a chemical imbalance in their brain. I do not hear that anymore, even though psychiatrists are still quick to prescribe anti-depressants.

To make matters worse, all specialties of doctors are prescribing these drugs, often misdiagnosing someone with depression when their problem is really anxiety. Also, psychiatrists in general are prescribing multiple drug therapies. It is not uncommon for one of my counselees to be on three, four, or five psychiatric medications. The problem with helping people come off their medications is not going away. It is getting worse and more complicated. I believe doctors are sincerely trying to help their patients and do care about them. Also, it is important to note that it is *not* a sin for your counselee to follow the doctor's orders. Even though we are *not* doctors, we need to know a few basic things about these drugs and how to counsel our counselees about them.

Categories of Anti-Depressants and Other Psychiatric Drugs

The most common category of anti-depressant is the "selective serotonin reuptake inhibitors" (SSRIs). These medications cause an increase in the level of serotonin in the fluid spaces in the brain. As I wrote earlier, the medicines accomplish that by changing the permeability of the cell wall so that the drug-targeted neurotransmitter can shift out of the cell but not shift back in. Therefore, the cell wall will not permit the *reuptake* of the neurochemical. So, the neurological cell is tricked into making more and more and shifting it into the fluid space. Also, keep in mind that every nerve cell in the body is affected, therefore some side effects have nothing to do with the brain. The most prescribed ones today are Zoloft, Celexa, Prozac, Trazadone, and Lexapro. Trazadone is also used to help patients sleep.

Another category of anti-depressants is the "serotonin *and* norepinephrine reuptake inhibitors" which target serotonin and norepinephrine. Three of the commonly used ones today are Effexor, Cymbalta, and Pristig. Cymbalta is also used to help patients with chronic pain. These can be more difficult to withdraw from as they affect two neurotransmitters instead of one.

There is an atypical category of anti-depressant, and it is a dopamine reuptake inhibitor. It is an older drug, but Wellbutrin is the most widely used one today. Often, if the patient is diagnosed as bi-polar, they will additionally be prescribed a mood stabilizer. Mood stabilizers calm the brain down and the most used ones today are Depakote, Lithium, Lamictil, Tegretol, and Sycrest.

Another category of drug that may be prescribed in addition to an anti-depressant is an anti-psychotic. Those are primarily used for patients diagnosed with schizophrenia or for someone who has had a psychotic break such as a bi-polar 1 patient. Commonly prescribed anti-psychotics today are Zyprexa and Abilify. Other anti-psychotics are Thorazine, Haldol, Trilafon, and Prolixin.

The last category of psychiatric drugs is tranquilizers (benzodiazepines). Their primary use is for anxiety, typically for a limited amount of time due to the risk of addiction. However, I have had several counselees who have been on a tranquilizer for years. In this category, the most prescribed today is Xanax. Others are Valium, Librium, Tranxene, Klonopin, and Lorazepam.

It is easy to see how counselees end up with multiple drugs therapies. But getting back to anti-depressants, let's consider the side-effects.

Counseling Helps to Safely Come Off Antidepressants

Side Effects of Antidepressants

Because antidepressants are stimulant medications, it is not surprising that counselees have increased anxiety, even to the extreme of panic attacks and paranoia. These are especially noticeable the first month of a new prescription or an increased dosage. Most psychiatrists begin their patients on a low dose and gradually increase it.

The antidepressants can cause sleeplessness and abnormal dreams. There is one particularly dangerous side effect and that is akathisia. The counselee experiences a severe restlessness to the point of desperation. They are agitated and suicidal. I have only seen this about four times in all my counseling years, but it is obviously dangerous. One counselee of mine that experienced this had been on a Prozac-type medication for two weeks. She had not been previously suicidal but became suicidal on the anti-depressant. She could no longer sit still in a counseling session, but would pace back and forth, wringing her hands. Since I recognized what was happening to her, I told her what I suspected. She decided to notify her doctor that she was discontinuing it. Afterwards, she gradually began to feel better and more normal.

Other side effects of antidepressants are fatigue, weakness, tremors, dizziness, light headedness, and difficulty in concentrating. Often, because of difficulty concentrating, I tell my counselees to read their assignments aloud, pray and ask God to help them comprehend what they are reading, and, if need be, read it several times over.

Gastrointestinal side effects are dry mouth, upset stomach, decreased appetite, nausea, and vomiting. At first, weight loss is quite common, but typically over a long period of time, weight gain becomes a problem. Sometimes people gain enormous amounts of weight.

Most counselees experience a decreased sex drive, and even impotence. Other physical symptoms can be sweating and blurred vision. I knew of one surgeon years ago that began to take Prozac but had to take himself off it because his vision became blurred. Others have trouble tolerating antidepressants because they develop abnormal heart rhythm problems. Some have hair loss, acne, dry skin, chest pain, runny nose, bleeding, blood pressure changes, bone pain, bursitis, breast pain, anemia, swelling, low blood sugar and low thyroid activity. Obviously, not everyone experiences all those side effects and most adjust to them after a few weeks, but antidepressants affect every nerve cell in your body. Hence, the different side effects.

Finally, there are the uncontrollable neurologic symptoms. The neurologic symptoms occur for those on antipsychotics. It is common these days for a doctor to add an antipsychotic medicine in addition to an anti-depressant. Those side effects, if they are going to occur, typically occur after a *long* time on antipsychotics. They are called "tics" and "tardive dyskinesias" or "TDs". When one of these appear, the counselee may have a twitching of their face such as an eye twitch which will not stop. They also may have a drooping mouth on one side much like what would happen due to a stroke. Probably the most upsetting TD is when the counselee cannot control their tongue from darting in and out of their mouth. Most of the time, their psychiatrist will take them off the antidepressant and antipsychotic when the neurologic side effects begin to appear. It may take several months for the side effect to go away, or in some cases, can be permanent.

Obviously, a biblical counselor could scare their counselees to death with these side effects. That is not my intent. My intent is for the counselor to be aware of what may be happening and, it is a judgment call, to perhaps explain to their counselee what *may* be happening. I think an exception would be if you think your counselee is experiencing akathisia or is suicidal. Then certainly tell them what you think may be happening and refer them right away to their psychiatrist or whatever physician prescribed the antidepressant.

When the Counselee is at Greatest Risk

The first month on an antidepressant or an increased dose of an antidepressant places the counselee at risk. They will likely begin experiencing side effects. The most dangerous ones to watch for are akathisia, uncontrollable leg movements, anxiety, and insomnia. It would not take long for someone already emotionally upset to feel overwhelmed and suicidal. They could very well act on those tendencies. Generally, if the counselee has been on an antidepressant for less than a month, she or he can quit taking it without withdrawal effects. Of course, they would need to notify their doctor.

Counselors need to also be aware that antidepressants carry a black box warning. The warning is for teenagers or young adults who are at increased risk for suicide when starting to take one of these drugs. Some doctors make a judgment call that the patient is at greater risk of suicide without the medication. I would be much more comfortable with a psychiatrist making that judgment call than with other categories of doctors.

The other period when the counselee is at greatest risk is when they are withdrawing from an antidepressant. The most common withdrawal effects from antidepressants are "anxiety, crying spells, fatigue, insomnia, irritability, dizziness, flu-like aches and pain, nausea, vomiting, headaches, tremors, and sensory abnormalities such as burning, tingling, or electric shock-like symptoms."[1] Counselees may become suicidal while withdrawing and some of the medications are slow to be metabolized out of the body. For instance, the onset of withdrawal symptoms from Prozac could take up to twenty-five days after stopping the drug and last up to fifty-six days.[2] If a counselee did not know this, they might think the psychiatric "disease" had returned. The newer antidepressants will metabolize out of your body sooner than Prozac, but the withdrawal is the same.

Paxil and Zoloft are the worst offenders in terms of sheer numbers of people affected by withdrawal reactions, because they are short acting and have been widely prescribed. Effexor is the worst offender in terms of the lightning speed with which it can cause withdrawal reactions, within hours of just one missed dose.[3] I remember that one counselee, while slowly withdrawing from Effexor with the help of her psychiatrist, went through an absolute nightmare getting off.

The first month of taking or increasing the dose of an antidepressant and the withdrawal period are the most dangerous times for the counselee to be overwhelmed and panic. So, where does that leave biblical counselors and how can we help?

---

[1] Glenmullen, Joseph. *The Antidepressant Solution.* (New York: Free Press, 2005), p. 120.

[2] Glenmullen, p.85.

[3] Glenmullen, p. 88-89.

How to Help the Counselee Come off their Medicine with their Doctor's Help

First, I recommend that you gather some data. Start with Dr. Joseph Glenmullen's fascinating book entitled *The Antidepressant Solution*.[4] Dr. Glenmullen is a Harvard trained M.D. and board-certified Psychiatrist. He does use antidepressants in select patient cases, but he also has helped many to come safely off their antidepressant. His book will help you to have some knowledge of how a counselee may come off their medication safely. Also, it will help you to be able to talk to the counselee and their doctor, if necessary, in an informed way.

Even if you never talk to your counselee about their medication, research it to see what it is used for and the possible side effects. This is not for the purpose of talking to your counselee about it, but if you think they may be having a side effect from the medication, you can tell them of the possibility and recommend they discuss it with their doctor. It will also help you to have an overall picture of what is happening with your counselee.

Give your counselee hope that for the Christian they *can* be controlled by the Holy Spirit. God will not give them more than they can bear (1 Corinthians 10:13). Tell them that modern medicine is a grace gift from God and, often, it is helpful with whatever we struggle with. Recommend that they continue with biblical counseling so that, by God's grace, their thoughts and emotions will stabilize, and they can have *joy* in giving God glory.

Teach your counselee a biblical view of sanctification and where their feelings come from (their heart—what they are thinking and desiring). They have THOUGHTS and then FEELINGS and then ACTIONS. As biblical counselors we help them with their thoughts (renewing their mind) and hold them accountable for their actions (loving God and loving others). Tell them they *can* honor God and show love to others despite how they *feel*. Ultimately, as they obey God and honor Him, their feelings will improve and be replaced with the peace of God.

---

[4] *The Antidepressant Solution*. (New York: Free Press 2005).

Counseling Helps to Safely Come Off Antidepressants

When you and your counselee agree they have progressed to the point of beginning to go off their antidepressant, tell her to talk to her doctor about tapering off and say to him, "I have been receiving biblical (or faith-based) counseling, and my counselor and I both think I am ready to begin tapering off the medication. Would you be willing to help me *slowly* taper off?" So far, in all these years of counseling, I have never had a doctor refuse, but if they did, I would want to know why because they may have a particularly good reason. The medical literature directs the doctor to cut the antidepressant dosage in half, wait two or three weeks, and then discontinue it. Dr. Glenmullen says that is way too fast for almost everyone! That has also been my experience with my counselees. If their doctor refuses, the counselee has the option of finding another doctor or, at least, obtaining a second opinion.

I like what Dr. Charles Hodges recommends that your counselee tell her doctor: "I have been in counseling for the past six months or a year, and I have made many changes in my life and I would like to know if I need to continue to take this medicine. Would you help me wean off so that I can take a vacation from it and see how I do?" Dr. Hodges does not think it necessary to tell the doctor what kind of counseling they received.

Teach your counselee the possible withdrawal effects he or she may experience so they will not panic if they experience such things as agitation, headaches, anxiety, electric-like zaps in different parts of their body or feel like they have the flu. If the counselee does experience those withdrawal effects, they will be less likely to panic as it happens if they know about it ahead of time and that the effects will subside eventually. If the doctor increases the dosage and the withdrawal effects subside, that is proof of the withdrawal causing the symptoms. One of my counselees felt like she had the flu and went to the doctor twice, but later learned it was from tapering off her antidepressant. If she had known that possibility ahead of time, it would have been easier for her.

If your counselee is having a hard struggle with tapering off the medication, perhaps the doctor could slow down or cut down on the amount of medication taper. Sometimes this is difficult as different medications come in differing strengths. Interestingly, Prozac also comes in a liquid so the taper could be small amounts.

Some counselees decide to take themselves off their medication. Strongly caution them against doing that! Carefully document what you told them in your counseling notes. If they insist, you might want to suggest that they read Dr. Glenmullen's book mentioned earlier, *The Antidepressant Solution*, before they take matters into their own hands. I would be afraid for one of my counselees to take this matter into her own hands. She needs to work with her doctor to safely and slowly taper off.

During the time she is tapering off, you may need to see her more often to encourage her and give her hope biblically. Neither she nor her doctor has done anything wrong or illegal, but the time may come that she desires to come off the medication and leave the side-effects behind. Become informed so that you can appropriately prepare her to talk to her doctor but be careful not to overstep the bounds of your training.

We have the good news of the Gospel, and we are persuaded of the sufficiency of the Word of God. God *has* given to us **"everything we need pertaining to life and godliness"** (2 Peter 1:3). We and our counselees should come to know the grace and the power of God. We have eternal, real, concrete hope. Modern medicine is, also, a kindness from God to us; but for your counselee the time may come when they are, by God's grace, emotionally stable and are ready to come off their medication. You need to be ready to help them appropriately with their doctor's help.

Conclusion

The psychiatric drugs come and go. They are often advertised by the drug companies as safe when they first come on the market. Later, some are found to be dangerous, and the drug companies quietly place a black box warning label in the drug literature. Psychiatrists have admitted that there is no chemical imbalance causing depression. We need to have the same assurance, especially because we have the *sure* Word of God **"restoring the soul"** (Psalm 19:7).

Chapter Three

Counseling Women to Have a Gentle and Quiet Spirit

Most Christians think that a woman who possesses a "gentle and quiet spirit" does not talk very much, speaks in soft tones, and (of course) whispers when she talks! I tried that and, with my personality, it did not work. I even considered taking a vow of silence, but that did not work either. That *really* did not work. What did work, however, was begging God to make me that kind of woman; although, as the saying goes, I am still a work in process.

My mother used to tell me that I was just like my daddy. Well, that was not a compliment because, at times, he would steam roll over people with his personality to get his way. When the Lord saved me over forty years ago, I became a Christian zealot/steamroller. I latched hold of the Gospel and was so thrilled with the good news that I assumed everyone else wanted to hear it, too. Thus, I proceeded to tell them! Not only did I tell them the Gospel, but I also wrongly assumed that everyone who thinks they are a Christian is actually a Christian. My "zeal without knowledge" went over like a lead balloon as one-by-one my best friends and family thought I had lost my mind. My anything but "gentle and quiet" spirit proved it.

Moving on, I discovered Bible doctrine. Bible doctrine is simply what the Scriptures teach about a particular subject such as the Trinity or the doctrine of sin. Everything for me was a "hill to die on." So, I proceeded to verbally fight to the death over doctrine that I do not even believe any more! People warned me, "You are coming on too strong." That sort of made me feel guilty, but, after all, I certainly was not going to compromise what I thought was the truth.

When I did feel guilty, I would sometimes remember that I was supposed to have a "gentle and quiet spirit." Then I would pray and ask God to change me, and I would resume whispering when I talked. Over these forty plus years, God has certainly changed me for the better, but as I stated earlier, I am still a work in progress.

One day I got tired of whispering when I talked, and I decided to really find out what a "gentle and quiet spirit" is. So, I did a study on the topic which included a careful reading of Matthew Henry's book, *A Quest for Meekness and Quietness of Spirit*. Matthew Henry was a Puritan pastor who knew the Scriptures inside and out. His book was so convicting that I could not read more than a page or two without stopping to pray, to confess, and sometimes to call someone to ask their forgiveness. The Lord used that study to show me what a "gentle and quiet spirit" really is. Surprisingly, it did not have anything to do with whispering. And this is what I concluded: A woman with a gentle and quiet spirit,

> 1. Accepts God's dealings with her as good. She does not contend nor dispute with God.
>
> 2. Is not given to anger or fear.

The key Scripture concerning a gentle and quiet spirit is in 1 Peter 3:3-4. The Apostle Peter, when he wrote to the Christians who were scattered throughout the Roman Empire because of persecution, included this special word for the ladies:

> **Do not let your adorning be external—braiding of hair and the putting on of gold jewelry or the clothing you wear—but let your adorning be the hidden person of the heart with the imperishable beauty of a gentle and quiet spirit, which in God's sight is very precious** (1 Peter 3:3-4).

So, very much wanting to be precious in God's sight and now understanding what "gentle and quiet" really means, the Lord helped me to develop biblical principles and a practical understanding of how, by God's grace, to become that kind of woman. That is what this chapter is about: defining "gentle and quiet spirit," understanding biblical principles, and giving practical tips to help counselees become that kind of woman (including an assessment tool for homework).

Counseling Women to Have a Gentle and Quiet Spirit

A Gentle Spirit is Precious in God's Sight

Since the "gentle spirit" that a woman is to have is in the context of 1 Peter 3:3-4, I would like to begin this chapter by explaining those two verses—phrase by phrase. In turn, you can teach your counselee.

> **Do not let your adorning be external—the braiding of hair and the putting on of gold jewelry, or the clothing you wear....** (v. 3).

The Roman world was famous for the ladies' beehive hairdos. They were amazingly large, and I suspect, gave them terrible headaches. We do not see many hair styles like that today, but many women *do* spend inordinate amounts of time and money on their quest for beauty. It is certainly all right to enjoy the freedom the Lord has given us in makeup and dress, but it should not be our only adornment. Peter, instead, wants ladies to rethink what true beauty is. He goes on to write,

> **... but let your adorning be the hidden person of the heart...** (v. 4).

Men and women, back in Peter's day, had been taught by the Pharisees that to be holy, you must be outwardly clean. They logically thought that avoiding eating with an unclean Gentile or ritualistically washing your hands before meals rendered you holy. When the Lord Jesus began to openly teach, He turned their thinking inside out. It was not your outward cleanliness, but what was in your heart that mattered.

The "heart" is simply who you are on the inside. In other words, it is what you think and desire. God's work of grace in our heart encompasses holy thoughts, words, desires, and actions. The Scriptures describe this heart-work as taking place in the "inward man" (Romans 7:22). How God supernaturally works in our "hidden hearts" is a miracle of His grace to us. Peter is telling us that the true beauty of a woman comes not from her outward appearance, but what is in her heart – what she thinks and desires. So, ladies, let your true beauty be what you are thinking on the inside. This is of eternal importance as Peter goes on to explain.

... with the imperishable beauty...

This kind of beauty is utterly amazing. It is eternal and cannot fade. It is not depraved or affected by the corruption in the world. It reminds me of what King David wrote when he described the **"beauty of the Lord's holiness"** (Psalm 27:4). It is of eternal worth because of the work that God has begun in us and promises to complete in eternity. He deserves all the glory and honor because of what our Lord Jesus accomplished by His death on the cross. This eternal, unfading beauty is shown in a Christian woman who has -

... a gentle and quiet spirit...

This is a woman who has been **"born again to a living hope through the resurrection of Jesus Christ from the dead..."** (1 Peter 1:3). She loves and trusts God with all her heart. She is tranquil and peaceable inside and out. *She accepts God's dealings with her as good. She does not contend or dispute with God. She is not given to anger or fear.* So, what does God think about this kind of woman?

... which in God's sight is very precious.

Precious is a wonderful word. It can mean valued, loved, cherished, or priceless. King David, in Psalm 139, wrote that God's thoughts were precious to him. King Solomon, in Proverbs 3:15, wrote that wisdom **"is more precious than jewels."** The Apostle Peter used the word *precious* several times in his letters to Christians undergoing persecution: their faith when tested and proven genuine is more **"precious than gold"** (1 Peter 1:7). Also, Peter reminded them that they had been ransomed **"with precious blood ... the blood of Christ"** (1 Peter 1:19); that Christ was **"rejected by men, but choice and precious in the sight of God"** (1 Peter 2:4); that Christ is the cornerstone and therefore He is a **"precious value for you who believe"** (1 Peter 2:7). Not only is Christ precious but also a woman with a gentle and quiet spirit is considered precious in the sight of God (1 Peter 3:4).

The reason that a woman's "gentle and quiet spirit" is precious to God cannot be anything other than the fruit shown in her life because of the grace-work of God. Her life is a **"sacrifice of praise to God"** for what He has done (Hebrews 13:15). In other words, she is a **"living sacrifice"** (Romans 12:1). She is precious to God because of *His* holiness imputed to her and *His* grace giving her a **"gentle and quiet spirit"** (1 Peter 3:4).

What Does a Gentle and Quiet Spirit Look Like in Your Counselee?[5]

Another word for gentle is meek. This word is closely related to humility. It is a grace gift from God to the believer, a fruit of the Holy Spirit in their lives (Galatians 5:22-23). This gentle/meek spirit is manifested in attitudes like being teachable, having a desire to learn, agreeing that God's precepts are right and good even if what God requires is not what you want or what you previously believed to be true.

Matthew Henry put it this way, "Meekness opens the ear to discipline, silences objections, and suppresses the rising of the carnal mind against the Word [of God], consenting to the law [of God] that it is good and esteeming all [God's] precepts to be 'right' even when they give the greatest check to flesh and blood."[6]

What this means is that a woman with a gentle spirit silently, in her heart, submits to the Word of God without complaining or becoming frustrated. Just think about that for a minute. I vividly remember as a new Christian reading the New Testament realizing that so many of my thoughts and actions had been wrong. In fact, I could hardly get through two or three verses without coming under conviction.

The only way a godly woman can silently submit to God as she goes through the myriad of minor aggravations of her day, much less if she encounters a large trial, is for her to know God's Word and love it, think about what the Bible says in her circumstances, and agree with it. One major help in silently submitting to God is to understand His providence.

---

[5] The principles in this chapter were adapted from Matthew Henry's book, *a Quest for Meekness and Quietness of Spirit* (Morgan, Pennsylvania: Soli Deo Gloria Publications, c.1700).

[6] Matthew Henry, p.19, adaptation mine.

Providence is the "continuing action of God by which He preserves the creation which He has brought into being and guides it to His intended purposes for it."[7] Providence is a wondrous truth as it tells us that God is actively and continually working in our life. Knowing that God is always working in our life means that we can confidently live by faith when circumstances are grievous and difficult.

God uses many means including tests and trials that are difficult. Often counselees come for help during these difficult circumstances. Teach them about Providence and that God is using our circumstances for our good to prune us, mold us into His image, and test our faith. The astounding thing is that even evil done to us by others can be turned to good through God's providence. Everything has a purpose. Given that God's ways are higher than ours, we are to trust Him and walk in obedient, grateful faith.

"Faith is the assurance of things hoped for, the conviction of things not seen" (Hebrews 11:1). In a practical way, this means we have confidence that nothing we go through is in vain. Consider Joseph whose brothers sold him into slavery. He was able to forgive them and say to them, **"As for you, you meant evil against me, but God meant it for good …"** (Genesis 50:20). For Joseph, life was about what God was actively doing in his life for His glory. For the counselee, it is the same or it *should* be the same.

Looking back on his life, Joseph could see God's Providential hand in all his circumstances. That is true for us today. We may not clearly see God's hand while we are currently in difficult circumstances, but ultimately, we will. The Apostle Paul expressed it this way:

> **"And we know that for those who love God** [those who love Him obey Him] **all things work together for good, for those who are called according to His purpose** [His purpose is to glorify Himself] **for those whom He foreknew he also predestined to be conformed to the image of His Son …"** (Romans 8:28-29, explanation mine, ESV).

---

[7] Millard J. Erickson, *Christian Theology* (Grand Rapids, Michigan: Baker Book House, 1985), p.387.

Counseling Women to Have a Gentle and Quiet Spirit

What Paul knew; Joseph knew. We can know the same thing. Therefore, we *can* silently submit to God's plan for our life and walk in obedient, grateful faith even if we cannot see or understand what is happening.

A woman with a gentle/meek spirit *does* accept God's dealings with her as good. In addition to silently submitting to God's plan for her life, her gentleness is shown towards others through prudently governing her own anger whenever anything occurs that is provoking. Martin Luther expressed it this way:

> Christians must not be sharp and bitter, but gentle, mild, courteous, and fair spoken, and such as make others to delight in their company. They can wink at other men's faults and will be well contented to yield and give place to others, contented to bear with those who are froward [unreasonable, difficult] and intractable, as someone said: "Thou must know the manner of thy friends, but thou must not hate them." Such a one was our Savior Christ. It is said of Peter that he wept often as he remembered the sweet mildness of Christ. It is an excellent virtue and most necessary in every kind of life.[8]

In his book, *A Quest for Meekness and Quietness of Spirit*, Matthew Henry explained what he called the "three great dictates of meekness." For our purposes, I have adapted the first two and added a third one of my own.

Directive Number One
Hear Reason

Some people simply do not take time to listen before they react. Mothers have been known to discipline the wrong child. Others regret decisions they have made without having all the available facts. Many people rudely interrupt others because they think they know what the other person is going to say. When anyone does those things,

---
[8] Martin Luther, *Commentary on Galatians* (Grand Rapids, Michigan: Fleming H. Revell, 1923), p.379.

they are described biblically as a fool. **"A fool takes no pleasure in understanding, but only in expressing his opinion"** (Proverbs 18:2, ESV). **"He who gives an answer before he hears, it is folly and shame to him."** (Proverbs 18:13). The Apostle James expressed it this way: **"Know this, my beloved brethren, let every person be quick to hear…"** (James 1:19, ESV). So before reacting, we are to listen. As Matthew Henry wrote, "Hear reason." That leads us to the second great dictate.

Directive Number Two
Keep Passion Silent

The Puritans called our emotions "natural passions." They are "natural" alright! Instead of naturally reacting, we should take time to think about what we want to say. At times, it would be good to say initially, "I need to think about what I want to say, and I will get back with you." You see, **"The heart of the righteous *ponders how to answer*, but the mouth of the wicked pours out evil things"** (Proverbs 15:28, emphasis added).

When Nehemiah left Persia and went back to Jerusalem to rebuild the wall, he met significant resistance from Sanballat and Tobiah the Ammonite who were verbally threatening and harassing Nehemiah, as well as oppressing the poor people in Jerusalem. It made Nehemiah angry. This is what he wrote:

> **"I was very angry when I heard their outcry and these words.** *I took counsel with myself,* **and I brought charges against the nobles and the official. I said to them, '… The thing that you are doing is not good. Ought you not to walk in the fear of our God …'"** (Nehemiah 5:6-9, emphasis added, ESV).

The point is that Nehemiah *thought about* what he wanted to say *before* he reacted. We need to do the same thing. When we do, that leads us to the third great dictate.

Counseling Women to Have a Gentle and Quiet Spirit

Directive Number Three
Trust that God will Give you Grace

There is an astounding promise to Christians in 1 Corinthians 10:13. I recommend you have all your counselees memorize it.

> **No temptation has overtaken you that is not common to man. God is faithful, and He will not let you be tempted beyond your ability, but with the temptation He will also provide the way of escape, that you may be able to endure it.**

What an incredible hope! We not only will *not* be tempted beyond our ability to resist, but we also will ultimately be given a way of escape. We do not *have* to respond sinfully.

Obviously, we still do sin, but when we do, we have an advocate with the Father. Often, when provoked, we feel irritated or frustrated. That means that we are angry. Knowing that God will not let us be tempted beyond what we can bear gives us great incentive to take the time to rethink what we were thinking that caused us to be angry. Instead, we should think a kind, tenderhearted, or forgiving thought (Ephesians 4:31-32). The Scriptures call this **"renewing your mind and taking your thoughts captive"** (Romans 12:1-2; 2 Corinthians 10:5). It is a way to put-off the old self and put-on the new self (Ephesians 4:22-24). With God helping you, you will be **"disciplining yourself for the purpose of godliness"** (1 Timothy 4:7).

I suggest that when my counselee feels frustrated or irritated, she is to write down what she is thinking. The emotions she feels are coming from her sinful heart. So, after she writes down what she is thinking, I then teach her to replace the sinful thought with a righteous, God-honoring thought. Here are several examples. On the left side of the chart are typical angry responses to provocations. On the right side of the chart is the gentle/meek thought or response.

Anger/ Natural Passions	**Meekness/ A Grace from God and an Obligation of Man to Respond Righteously**
"That irritates me!"	"I am being providentially hindered and must stop and thank God for the interruption. God is good and He has a purpose in this." (Romans 8:28-29, 1 Thessalonians 5:18)
Yell at the children in anger because they are bickering.	Reminds self: "**The anger of man does not achieve the righteousness of God.**" (James 1:19) "I need to help each child take the beam out of their own eye." Sit them down and ask each one individually "What have you done wrong in this incident?" (Matthew 7:1-5) Then appropriately correct and/or discipline each child individually.
Become too intense and harsh in tone of voice with friend who does not agree doctrinally with me.	Reminds self that when dealing with doctrinal error "**the Lord's bondservant gently corrects those that are in opposition...**" (2 Timothy 2:23-26) Remember how far God has brought me. (1Thessalonians 5:14; 2 Timothy 4:2) Then speak in a calm, gentle tone of voice.
Feeling frustrated and aggravated with a slow driver when you are in a hurry. Thinking, "Hurry up, get out of the way!" Slam hand on steering wheel.	Says to self, "Lord thank you for testing me this morning and reminding me that you are in control."

In Ecclesiastes 7:9, King Solomon wrote, **"Do not be eager in your heart to be angry, for anger resides in the bosom of fools."** Matthew Henry referred to that verse in the following quote:

Counseling Women to Have a Gentle and Quiet Spirit

> Meekness is forward to forgive injuries and put up affronts, and has some excuse or other ready wherewith to extenuate and qualify the provocation which an angry man will industriously aggravate. While the world so full of the sparks of provocation, and there is so much tinder in the hearts of the best, no marvel if anger comes sometimes into the bosom of a wise man, but it rests only in the **'bosom of fools'** (Ecclesiastes 7:9).[9]

A woman with a gentle/meek heart will think about what she should be thinking and how she should respond. By God's enabling grace, she can prudently govern her anger when she is provoked. She will grow and mature in God's grace, and He will use her meekness to teach and enable her to patiently bear the anger of others.

King David was distressed due to his enemies. In Psalm 39:12, ESV, he said, **"I will guard my ways, that I may not sin with my tongue; I will guard my mouth with a muzzle, so long as the wicked are in my presence."** When he did speak, he spoke to the Lord, **"Hear my prayer, O LORD; and give ear to my cry…!"** (Psalm 39:1,12).

David was referring to his enemies and the enemies of God's kingdom. Someone does not have to be our enemy or an unbeliever for us to be provoked. Often, instead of being impatient, we need to muzzle our mouths. Simply say to yourself, "Lord forgive me for being angry. Your Word tells me that love is patient. I *can* show love to this person by patiently listening. Lord help me to think a patient and kind thought." Matthew Henry put it this way, "Better to yield by silence to our brother…than by angry speaking to yield to the devil…who will ever be our sworn enemy."[10]

Keep in mind that we have been talking about a woman with a gentle/meek spirit. She is not given to anger and she graciously submits herself to God's Providential care over her. She does not contend nor dispute with God. She accepts God's dealings with her as good. Now we want to turn briefly to what is a quiet spirit.

---

[9] Matthew Henry, page 30.

[10] Matthew Henry, page 35.

A Quiet Spirit

It might be easier to begin with what a quiet spirit is not. It is not whispering when you talk or not having an opinion. Instead, it means you are not given to anger or fear. In other words, you trust God and there is a corresponding tranquility in your soul. As a result, you have a calming effect on others and especially on your family. A woman with a quiet spirit looks forward to what God is going to do in her life. She is like the Proverbs 31 wife whose **"strength and dignity are her clothing, and she laughs at the time to come. She opens her mouth with wisdom, and the teaching of kindness is on her tongue"** (Proverbs 31:25-26, ESV).

She does not fret about the "what ifs?" Instead, she **"makes her requests known to God with thanksgiving"** (Philippians 4:6-7). In her dependence and humility before God, she **"cast[s] all [her] anxieties on Him, because** [she knows and remembers] **that He cares for [her]"** (1 Peter 5:7, explanation mine).

Matthew Henry noted the nature of such a Christian woman:

> A quiet soul even if provoked does not fret at all, nor perplex itself with anxious cares but composes itself to make the best of that which is. This quietness is a good step taken towards the **"mature man, to the measure of the stature of the fullness of Christ"** (Ephesians 4:13).[11]

Only God can make you and your counselee to be women with a **"gentle and quiet spirit"** (1 Peter 3:4). That is true beauty, unfading, and eternal. This is how the holy women of old who hoped in God used to adorn themselves (1 Peter 3:5). Ask your counselee questions such as: "Do you want to be a woman like this? Do you want to be considered very precious in God's sight? (1 Peter 3:4).

Do you want to honor the Lord in that way after all that He has done for you? If so, begin by praying and sincerely asking that God will make you into that kind of woman. Then, follow up with a careful biblical assessment of how, by God's enabling grace, you need to

---

[11] Matthew Henry, page 45.

change. To help your counselee make that biblical assessment of her life, assign the following homework and tell her to take her time and prayerfully work through it.

Just How Gentle and Quiet Am I?

Instructions:

- *Carefully* read each of the following questions or statements.
- Circle the numbers of those on which you need to work.
- Go back to those you circled, look up the Scriptures, memorize them. Learn them so well that you can easily say them.
- Spend time in prayer and thinking about how, by God's grace, you need to change.
- Show the list to your family and close friends and ask them to hold you accountable when they observe you not having a gentle and quiet spirit.

Keep in mind that a woman with a "gentle and quiet spirit" accepts God's dealings with her as good. She does not contend or dispute with God. She is not given to anger or fear.

1. Am I more likely to think "This makes me angry!" or "What might God be doing in this situation?"?

    A man's discretion makes him slow to anger, and it is his glory to overlook a transgression (Proverbs 19:11).

2. What would more likely come to mind: "Love is patient. I can respond in a kind way and give glory to God." Or "This irritates me!"?

    Love is patient, love is kind and is not jealous; love does not brag and is not arrogant, does not act unbecomingly; it does not seek its own, is not provoked... (1 Corinthians 13:4-7).

3. Which describes how you would likely react: sighing and withdrawing in anger, or in gentleness trying to help the other person to understand?

> **So, as those who have been chosen of God, holy and beloved, put on a heart of compassion, kindness, humility, gentleness and patience; bearing with one another, and forgiving each other, whoever has a complaint against anyone; just as the Lord forgave you, so also should you** (Colossians 3:12-13).

4. Do you ever stop and ask yourself?

   - Why am I angry?
   - Why am I so terribly angry?
   - Why am I angry at all?
   - What reason is there for all this emotion?
   - Should I be reacting so strongly because of such a sudden and transient provocation?

   > **Do nothing from selfishness or empty conceit** [your own vain glory], **but with humility of mind regard one another as more important than yourselves; do not merely look out for your own personal interests, but also for the interests of others** (Philippians 2:3-5, explanation mine).

   > **But flee from these things, you man of God, and pursue righteousness, godliness, faith, love, perseverance, and gentleness** (1 Timothy 6:11).

5. While angry, do you ever reveal secrets, slander, make rash vows, make railing accusations, use reviling language, call names, or take God's name in vain?

   > **Remind them to be subject to rulers, to authorities, to be obedient, to be ready for every good deed, to malign no one, to be peaceable, gentle, showing every consideration for all men** (Titus 3:1-2).

6. Are you more likely to play angry thoughts over and over in your mind, or to give the other person a blessing by praying for them?

> **Let all bitterness and wrath and anger and clamor and slander be put away from you, along with all malice. Be kind to one another, tender-hearted, forgiving each other, just as God in Christ also has forgiven you** (Ephesians 4:31-32).

7. Are you rightfully defending yourself when unjustly accused? Or are you proud and quarreling?

> **For this finds favor, if for the sake of conscience toward God a person bears up under sorrows when suffering unjustly. For what credit is there if, when you sin and are harshly treated, you endure it with patience? But if when you do what is right and suffer for it you patiently endure it, this finds favor with God.** (1 Peter 2:19-23).

8. Is it easy for you to acknowledge your error, or do you insist upon your own vindication?

> **…and all of you, clothe yourselves with humility toward one another, for God is opposed to the proud, but gives grace to the humble** (1 Peter 5:5).

9. Will you listen to and consider someone else's reproof of you even if they are your inferior (such as your child), or do you bully them and blame them?

> **Commit your way to the LORD, trust also in Him, and He will do it. He will bring forth your righteousness as the light and your judgment as the noonday. Rest in the LORD and wait patiently for Him; do not fret because of him who prospers in his way, because of the man who carries out wicked schemes. Cease from anger and forsake wrath, do not fret, it leads only to evildoing** (Psalm 37:5-8).

10. Do you struggle greatly with difficult emotions such as anxiety or frustration during the days before your menstrual period? Is it likely your entire family will know your hormones are acting up?

> **Your adornment must not be merely external – braiding the hair, and wearing gold jewelry, or putting on dresses; but let it be the hidden person of the heart, with the imperishable quality of a gentle and quiet spirit, which is precious in the sight of God** (1 Peter 3:3-4).

11. Do you think calm thoughts, or are you disturbed within?

> **Who among you is wise and understanding? Let him show by his good behavior his deeds in the gentleness of wisdom** (James 3:13).

12. Do you deal gently with others in patience and compassion, or are you hard and unforgiving?

> **…bearing with one another, and forgiving each other, whoever has a complaint against anyone; just as the Lord forgave you, so also should you** (Colossians 3:13).

> **Let your gentle spirit be known to all men. The Lord is near** (Philippians 4:5).

13. Do you enjoy life and love life, or do you dread each day and fret and worry?

> **Be anxious for nothing, but in everything by prayer and supplication with thanksgiving let your requests be made known to God. And the peace of God, which surpasses all comprehension, will guard your hearts and your minds in Christ Jesus** (Philippians 4:6-7).

14. Are you easily provoked or slow to anger?

   > **She opens her mouth in wisdom, and the teaching of kindness is on her tongue** (Proverbs 31:26).

15. Are your thoughts calm and rational, or do you sometimes overreact to circumstances?

   > **... and walk in love, just as Christ also loved you and gave Himself up for us, an offering and a sacrifice to God as a fragrant aroma** (Ephesians 5:2).

   > **Beloved, I urge you as aliens and strangers to abstain from fleshly lusts which wage war against the soul. Keep your behavior excellent among the Gentiles, so that in the thing in which they slander you as evildoers, they may because of your good deeds, as they observe them, glorify God in the day of visitation** (1 Peter 2:11-12).

16. Are you more like the high priest in Hebrews 5:1-2 who has compassion on the ignorant and those going astray (since he is also subject to weakness), or more like the wicked servant in Matthew 18:21-35 who would not have compassion and pity on his fellow servant?

   > **For every high priest taken from among men is appointed on behalf of men in things pertaining to God, in order to offer both gifts and sacrifices for sin; he can deal gently with the ignorant and misguided, since he himself also is beset with weakness ...** (Hebrews 5:1-2).

17. Do you forebear (put up with others), or are you easily provoked for small cause?

   > **But He, being compassionate, forgave their iniquity and did not destroy them; and often He restrained His anger and did not arouse all His wrath** (Psalm 78:38-39).

Let your gentle spirit be known to all men. The Lord is near (Philippians 4:5).

18. Are you fiery and hasty with what you say, or do you take great care to *think* about how to respond?

    Let no unwholesome word proceed from your mouth, but only such a word as is good for edification according to the need of the moment, so that it will give grace to those who hear. Do not grieve the Holy Spirit of God, by whom you were sealed for the day of redemption (Ephesians 4:29-30).

    What is the source of quarrels and conflicts among you? Is not the source your pleasures that wage war in your members? (James 4:1).

19. Do you use anger and threats to manipulate those under your authority, or do you give instruction in love?

    They also provoked Him to wrath at the waters of Meribah, so that it went hard with Moses on their account; because they were rebellious against his Spirit, he spoke rashly with his lips (Psalm 106:32-33).

20. Do you err on the side of mercy when correcting those under your authority, or are you harsh?

    The LORD is compassionate and gracious, slow to anger and abounding in lovingkindness ... For He Himself knows our frame; He is mindful that we are but dust (Psalm 103:8,14).

21. Do you treat others as you wish to be treated, or do you treat them with contempt?

    In everything, therefore, treat people the same way you want them to treat you, for this is the Law and the Prophets (Matthew 7:12).

22. Do you grumble and complain at your present circumstances that disappoint you, or are you grateful to God for what He is doing?

> **... and to make it your ambition to lead a quiet life and attend to your own business and work with your hands, just as we commanded you, so that you will behave properly toward outsiders and not be in any need** (1 Thessalonians 4:11).

> **I know how to get along with humble means, and I also know how to live in prosperity; in any and every circumstance I have learned the secret of being filled and going hungry, both of having abundance and suffering need** (Philippians 4:12).

23. Are you quick to imagine injuries, or do you assume the best about others unless proven otherwise?

> **Love ... bears all things, believes (the best) all things, hopes all things, endures all things. Love never fails ...** (1 Corinthians 13:7-8).

24. Are you envious of the wicked, or are you placing your trust in God?

> **Whom have I in heaven but You? And besides You, I desire nothing on earth. My flesh and my heart may fail, but God is the strength of my heart and my portion forever. For, behold, those who are far from You will perish; You have destroyed all those who are unfaithful to You. But as for me, the nearness of God is my good; I have made the Lord GOD my refuge, that I may tell of all Your works** (Psalm 73:25-28).

25. Are you becoming more aware of times when you are not gentle with others, or you are disputing with God, or do you see no need to change in this area of your life?

> **Therefore, let him who thinks he stands take heed**

that he does not fall (1 Corinthians 10:12).

26. A reproof is telling another person that what they are doing or saying is wrong. When it is necessary to reprove another person, are you more likely to lash out impulsively or gently try to help them to turn from their sin with good will, soft words, and objective arguments?

    Brethren, even if anyone is caught in any trespass, you who are spiritual, restore such a one in a spirit of gentleness... (Galatians 6:1).

27. Do you pray and ask the Lord to make you a gentle woman, or does it not cross your mind?

    Ask, and it will be given to you; seek, and you will find; knock, and it will be opened to you. For everyone who asks receives, and the one who seeks finds, and to the one who knocks it will be opened. Or which one of you, if his son asks him for bread, will give him a stone? Or if he asks for a fish, will give him a serpent? If you then, who are evil, know how to give good gifts to your children, how much more will your Father who is in heaven give good things to those who ask him!" (Matthew 7:7-11, ESV).

28. Do you brood and become angry when you are persecuted for your faith, or do you rejoice that the Lord counted you worthy to suffer for His sake?

    Blessed are you when people insult you and persecute you, and falsely say all kinds of evil against you because of Me. Rejoice and be glad, for your reward in heaven is great; for in the same way they persecuted the prophets who were before you (Matthew 5:11-12).

    So they [Peter and the Apostles] went on their way from the presence of the Council, rejoicing that they

> had been considered worthy to suffer shame for His name (Acts 5:41).
>
> I said, "I will guard my ways that I may not sin with my tongue; I will guard my mouth as with a muzzle while the wicked are in my presence (Psalm 39:1).

29. Do you become aggravated, hurt, or frustrated with God over your circumstances or do you have great joy in serving Him on His terms?

> Woe to the one who quarrels with his Maker—an earthenware vessel among the vessels of earth! Will the clay say to the potter, "What are you doing?" Or the thing you are making say, "He has no hands?" (Isaiah 45:9).
>
> The foolishness of man ruins his way, and his heart rages against the LORD (Proverbs 19:3).

Conclusion

Follow up with your counselee to see how she did on her study. Almost everyone finds areas that they need to work on. Ask her, "Have you prayed and asked God to help you? Have you come up with a biblical plan of action to study the areas that you know you are weak in and how, by God's grace, to change?" Tell her about good books and resources to further her study.

Encourage her that Scripture tells us that we can confidently go to God when we struggle with temptation because our Lord Jesus sympathizes with our weaknesses, and He will help us.

> Since then we have a great high priest who has passed through the heaven, Jesus, the Son of God, let us hold fast our confession. For we do not have a high priest who is unable to sympathize with our weaknesses, but one who in every respect has been

tempted as we are, yet without sin. Let us then with confidence draw near to the throne of grace, that we may receive mercy and find grace to help in time of need (Hebrews 4:14-16, ESV).

The Apostle Paul exhorted his readers in Philippi that,

> **...** *it is God who works in you, both to will and to work for his good pleasure.* **Do all things without grumbling or deceiving, that you may be blameless and innocent, children of God without blemish in the midst of a crooked and twisted generation, among whom you shine as lights in the world, holding fast to the word of life, so that in the day of Christ I may be proud that I did not run in vain or labor in vain** (Philippians 2:13-16, emphasis added, ESV).

Encourage your counselee to pray dependently for help and, when she gets up off her knees, get to work at renewing her mind and changing her actions.

> **"Have nothing to do with irreverent, silly myths. Rather,** *train yourself for godliness***, for while bodily training is of some value, godliness is of value in every way, as it holds promise for the present life and also for the life to come. The saying is trustworthy and deserving of full acceptance. For** *to this end we toil and strive, because we have our hope set on the living God,* **who is the Savior of all people, especially of those who believe"** (1Timothy 4:7-10, emphasis added, ESV).

A gentle and quiet spirit does not happen naturally or automatically. It is an amazing gift from God. As a woman matures as a Christian, she *will* dispute less and less with God and be more and more content and grateful for her life and circumstances. She will trust God more and more and she will be less angry and fearful. She can become a uniquely beautiful woman, glorifying God in her heart.

Do not let your adorning be external—the braiding of hair and the putting on of gold jewelry, or the clothing you wear—but let your adorning be the hidden person of the heart with the imperishable beauty of a gentle and quiet spirit, which in God's sight is very precious (1 Peter 3:3-4).

Biblical Counseling in Practice

Chapter Four

Counseling Women Who are Deeply Emotionally Disturbed

In the weeks preceding my salvation, I was what I would now characterize as a person deeply disturbed. I was emotionally unstable, had frequent dark morbid thoughts, at times those thoughts were suicidal. Some people turn to cutting for relief from the overwhelming emotional pain, but I turned to alcohol. I remember one day thinking perhaps God was punishing me, and the anxiety I experienced was so extreme it overwhelmed me. I thought I would die.

I remember a conversation I had with our friend, Ed Sherwood, and he asked me, "Are you a Christian?" I told him, "No, and if I died today, I would go to hell." The sin in my life was shameful and wicked. Several friends had witnessed to me and convinced me that what I deserved was hell. Out of desperation, I began to read the Bible. Ed suggested that I read the Gospel of John over and over and pray for God to help me. So, I quit drinking and started reading. I would read the entire thing at one sitting, sometimes several times in one day. I also started praying and asking God to help me.

After being in emotional agony for weeks with extreme anxiety, one night while reading the Gospel of John, God had mercy on me and saved my soul. He forgave my sin and gave me a new heart with new desires. Those desires included a love for His Word and a desire to serve Him however He chose. He gave me His peace. The dark morbid thoughts were replaced with an incredible joy in the Lord and a longing for Him. He changed me from a person who hated to say the name of Jesus to one who loved hearing His name, thinking about Him, longing for Him, and telling others about Him.

In this chapter, I want to help you biblically counsel others who are like I was. I began to have an interest in this subject while I was working as a counselor to women at the Atlanta Biblical Counseling Center with Lou Priolo. Over my thirty plus years as a counselor to women, I believe there were only a few women I would place in this category, but there were enough that I began to see patterns of their thinking and behavior. So, I want to share with you seven characteristics of a counselee who is, what I would term, "deeply disturbed" and some practical, biblical counseling tips for each of the characteristics.

Definition of a Deeply Emotionally Disturbed Counselee

I am defining a deeply disturbed counselee as one with a combination of sin patterns in her life and as a result, she is emotionally unstable, often to the point of suicidal thoughts and self-harm. She is on a downward spiral. It reminds me of Romans Chapter one that describes God turning people over to their own sin. Often, she will turn to self-injury such as cutting, burning, or hitting herself to be distracted from the emotional pain. She also may turn to alcohol, medication, or illegal drugs to help distract her from her pain.

The counselees I have described were different people with quite different backgrounds, but they had two characteristics in common: (1) they were not persuaded of God's goodness and (2) they were not grateful to God.

The sin patterns I am about to describe are not something that should require years of biblical counseling to overcome. If the counselee tells you she is a Christian and gives a biblical answer to questions about her salvation, assume that she is, but expect her to repent. Coming to counseling and doing her homework is not necessarily a sign of repentance. True repentance is a whole U-turn in her heart. True repentance is a grace gift from God. The Word of God is alive and powerful, and if she truly knows God, His Word will have a supernatural effect on her. (See Hebrews 4:12).

Sometimes women who are deeply emotionally disturbed experienced some sort of terrible trauma as a child or young adult. She may have been sexually molested or beaten unmercifully, her parents may have bitterly divorced, or one of her parents may have died. It seems to be especially difficult if *both* parents were mean, cruel people. The sin against her may have been exceedingly vile and your heart will go out to her.

Counseling Women Who are Deeply Emotionally Disturbed

There have been times I was exceptionally long-suffering with a woman who was abused. However, I have come to realize that letting them continue in the same old sin patterns is not love. It is unbiblical mercy. It is ultimately unkind as you are in a sense condoning their sin. Patiently teach them, exhort them in a kind tone of voice, give them hope, but call them to repentance. Pray that God will grant it to them.

Counselees who cut themselves are undergoing great emotional pain. It could be for any one and probably a combination of reasons. Cutting is highly addictive. The thought is that the physical pain releases endorphins into the brain and gives a natural high. No known medicine is helpful to quell the urge, but often the patient is treated with antidepressants and antianxiety medications. The secular therapists recommend talk therapy, meditation, art, yoga, and/or exercise. The consequences of cutting are scarring, possible infections, subsequent hospitalizations, and even death. Cutting is also a gateway to suicide.

Not all persons who are deeply emotionally disturbed are cutters, but they do have common characteristics. In this chapter, I have identified seven. The first one is anger.

The Common Characteristic of Anger

A lot of people struggle with anger but for the person deeply emotionally disturbed, their anger is an intense resentment. Often, they have thoughts like, "I hate…" or "I despise …" It is common for them to wish horrific things would happen to others. This anger goes beyond the usual, "I'm irritated." It is malicious and cruel and vengeful. When you attempt to exhort them to do and think rightly, they often become belligerent and even threatening.

Biblical Counseling Tips

Assign your counselee a "self-talk log." Explain to her that this is not a journal on how she feels but a list of her thoughts when she is experiencing emotional pain. Do not be surprised at how bad the thoughts are. For example, "I hate him. I wish he were dead." Or "I wish something bad would happen to him." "I despise her!"

As a counselor, carefully go over each thought and take her to Scripture to "renew her mind." Teach her the biblical concept of "Putting off and Putting on" from Ephesians 4:22-24.[12] Correct the thoughts one-by-one. For example, change "I wish something bad would happen to him" to "Lord, I pray that you will show yourself kind to him and grant him repentance from his selfishness."

Teach her the biblical concept of loving others. That includes her enemies, her neighbors, her coworkers, her family, and her counselor! Explain in detail Matthew 22:35-40. This is the Lord Jesus speaking here and the Pharisees are trying to trick Him. The question is not surprising as it was common for them to think in terms of greater and lesser laws. The greater ones they believed you had to keep, but the lesser laws were optional in their minds. How convenient for them because they were the ones to determine what they thought were the greater and lesser laws. So, read the Matthew passage and explain it to your counselee.

> **One of them a lawyer, asked Him a question, testing Him, "Teacher, which is the great commandment in the Law?" And He said to him, "You shall love the LORD your God with all your heart, and with all your soul, and with all your mind.** [One way love for God is shown is by obeying His Word not just outwardly but in your heart, what you are thinking]. **This is the great and foremost commandment. The second is like it, You shall love your neighbor as yourself."** [To love others is to be kind, patient, not provoked, etc. See 1 Corinthians 13:4-7. It is a given that we love ourselves even if our focus is to disparage ourselves.] (Matthew 22:35-39, explanation mine).

---

[12] For a free downloadable copy of Martha's study, see her blog site: marthapeacetew@blogspot.com.

In addition, show your counselee John's warning in 1 John about her salvation.

> **On the other hand, I am writing a new commandment to you, which is true in Him and in you, because the darkness is passing away and the true Light is already shining. The one who says he is in the Light and yet hates his brother is in the darkness until now. The one who loves his brother abides in the Light and there is no cause for stumbling in him. But the one who hates his brother is in the darkness and walks in the darkness and does not know where he is going because the darkness has blinded his eyes** (1 John 2:7-11).

Be patient yet clear about her sin. You want to get to her heart and that is what God's Word does. Another characteristic of a person who is deeply emotionally disturbed is fear.

The Common Characteristic of Fear

Counselees like this are often overwhelmed with fear. It can be extreme such as full-blown panic attacks. When she experiences a panic attack, she becomes so frightened that adrenalin (epinephrine) is secreted into her blood stream from the adrenal glands located on top of her kidneys. Her heart will pound, her hands shake, she will feel as if she cannot breathe, and think she is going to die. Often, her greatest fear then becomes the fear itself. If she begins to hyperventilate, she will eventually faint because of breathing out too much carbon dioxide. After fainting, she will begin to breathe again and wake up. Encourage her to take slow breaths to stop that process from happening.

I would assign her to complete a self-talk log writing down her thoughts when she feels anxious. Next, I would teach her how to do an anxiety journal based on Philippians 4:6-9. For details, see chapter nine of this book. Also, Jay Adams has written an excellent pamphlet on overcoming fear, "What Do You Do When FEAR Overcomes

You?"[13] She would need to read it for homework and choose several points that stand out to her. Be prepared to go over those points in the next counseling session. In addition, if she is having trouble functioning in life, I would make a list of her responsibilities such as prepare a simple meal for her family and to get out of the bed by 7:00 AM and take her shower and get dressed. Exhort her to fulfill her responsibilities whether she feels like it or not.

The Common Characteristic of a Blasphemous View of God

Often, a counselee who is deeply emotionally disturbed will have blasphemous views of God. Her thoughts may be that God is not good, or that He has malice towards her and is unfair. She may even hate God because of things that have happened to her in the past or are happening in the present. This characteristic will plummet a counselee very quickly into the depths of despair, and in her desperation, she may harm herself.

Teach her the biblical concept of mind renewal. Her thoughts are exceedingly wicked and God is greatly offended. She must change her mind and begin thinking God-honoring thoughts.

> **And do not be conformed to this world, but be transformed by the renewing of your mind, so that you may discern what the will of God is, that which is good and acceptable and perfect** (Romans 12:2).

Her pride and anger are causing her to have a very unbiblical and low view of God and a high view of herself. It is imperative that you immerse her in a solid study of the attributes of God. I highly recommend Arthur Pink's book, *The Attributes of God*. Also, I recommend my book, *Precious Truths in Practice*. In addition, Romans 2:4 certainly applies in her situation: **"Or do you think lightly of the riches of His kindness and tolerance and patience, not knowing that the kindness of God leads you to repentance?"**

---

[13] Adams, Jay. "What Do You Do When Fear Overcomes You?" (Phillipsburg, NJ: P&R Publishing).

Point her to a high view of God and thinking rightly about Him. Exhort her to repent and change her mind about God, to sincerely ask His forgiveness, and to start expressing thankfulness to Him. Her emotional stability is at stake and so is her eternal soul. Take as much time as needed to exhort her from a blasphemous view of God to a high and holy view of our sovereign God.

The Common Characteristic of Not Being Grateful

A quite common characteristic of a counselee who is deeply emotionally disturbed that is associated with the previous one is that she is not grateful. She believes she deserves better. She thinks she is somehow getting a raw deal, and she does not thank God. Even the good things that happen to her are not enough.

Teach her the story of the children of Israel grumbling in the wilderness. Explain how God is greatly grieved at their ingratitude especially after all that He did for them bringing them out of slavery in Egypt. See Exodus 15:22 through Exodus 17:7. It is not just in the Old Testament that God does not want His people to grumble and complain, it applies to us today. We are told to *be thankful* regardless of our circumstances.

> **Let the peace of Christ rule in your hearts, to which indeed you were called in one body; and *be thankful*. Let the word of Christ richly dwell within you, with all wisdom teaching and admonishing one another with psalms and hymns and spiritual songs, *singing with thankfulness in your hearts to God*. Whatever you do in word or deed, do all in the name of the Lord Jesus, *giving thanks* through Him to God the Father** (Colossians 3:15-17, emphasis mine).

> **Rejoice always; pray without ceasing; *in everything give thanks*; for this is God's will for you in Christ Jesus** (1 Thessalonians 5:16-18, emphasis mine).

Help your counselee come up with some emergency thoughts to think when she is struggling. Keep them simple and short, have her memorize them, and recite them to you at her next counseling session:

- Thank you, Lord, for the difficultly I am having.
- Thank you for reminding me how much I need You.
- Help me to honor You.
- No matter how *I* feel, *You* are good and faithful.

I would also teach her the chapter on the "Goodness of God" in the book, *Precious Truths in Practice*.[14] Encourage her to affirm God's goodness. Remind her to confess her ungrateful thoughts as sin and to renew her mind by thinking grateful thoughts. Explain that God is pruning her (not letting her be comfortable in her sin), and He has been long-suffering with her. Her trials are special opportunities to glorify Him.

The Common Characteristic of Trance-like Racing Thoughts

If your counselee reaches the point of having racing thoughts, she probably is not sleeping; and her emotional pain is so great that she feels as if she cannot bear the pain. Not sleeping is a bad sign. She most likely will become suicidal or self-abasing perhaps with cutting or hurting herself physically in some way, or she may direct her rage at someone else. She could take a weapon of some sort and hurt someone else.

At this point, you *must* take action and do whatever is necessary to protect her and her family. Notify her family and the elders in her church that she is in peril. Perhaps either her family or her elders in her church will arrange for someone to temporarily keep her children. I would call in two or more witnesses and verbally confront and warn her but do it calmly and very gently (see Matthew 18:15-18).

If she will not repent and is a danger to herself or others, take her to a psychiatric hospital for a psychiatric evaluation. If she refuses to go to the psychiatric hospital but will go to the emergency room, take her

---

[14] Peace, Martha. *Precious Truths in Practice* (Bemidji, MN. Focus Publishing, 2019).

there. They will conduct a psychiatric evaluation and send her on to the psychiatric hospital. If she refuses, call the police. Because it is against the law to threaten or commit suicide or homicide, (Romans 13:1) the police will take her to the emergency room even if it is against her will. Of course, we would prefer to not have to do that, but she and the people around her need to be protected. The police and laws are one of the ways that God protects us.

The Common Characteristic of Suspicion of Others

One of the characteristics of a person deeply emotionally disturbed is suspicion of others. In a case like this, the counselee easily judges motives of others misperceiving words or actions. Their assumption is that the other person is out to deliberately hurt them or make them look foolish.

Teach her why it is wrong to judge other people's motives. Only God can know what a person is thinking. So, unless the person tells us what they are thinking, we must give them the benefit of the doubt. The following Scripture is especially helpful:

> **Therefore, do not go on passing judgment before the time, but wait until the Lord comes who will both bring to light the things hidden in the darkness and disclose the motives of men's hearts; and then each man's praise will come to him from God** (1 Corinthians 4:5).

In the above passage, Paul is explaining that there are two things we are forbidden to judge: hidden things and men's motives. A hidden thing would be something you could not prove or know for sure. A person's motive is why they did or said what they did. When the Lord Jesus comes back a second time, He will make all those judgments. Meanwhile, we are to assume the best about others by thinking true and right thoughts. (Philippians 4:8).

Characteristic of Being Out of Touch with Reality

Your counselee may experience hallucinations, act on misperceptions as if they were real, be unable to sleep due to ungodly thoughts and guilt over sin. When I was in nursing school, I was assigned to a state psychiatric hospital for part of my training. I was not a Christian back then, and I considered that all those people had a disease no matter what their issue was. We were taught Sigmund Freud's psychiatric model. One patient stands out in my mind because she seemed to be perfectly normal. However, she took me aside one day to share with me her "secret." She said, "I gave birth to the Christ child, and I have radio tubes in my ovaries to communicate directly with God." Well, even as an unbeliever, I knew that was not true! So, I replied to her what I had been taught, "How do you *feel* about that?" It is sad that I did not help her to face reality.

If your counselee is out of touch with reality, tell her the truth but do it in love. Deep-seated delusions feel very real to her. Show her in the Scriptures how she is to think and what she is to believe. Exhort her to face reality but with a hope in God. For example, "This seems real, but the Scriptures tell me it is not. I must believe God."

In Titus chapter two, the older women are to teach and admonish the younger women. One of the mandates is for the young woman to be sensible. The Greek word for sensible is a broad term, and it means to help her have a sound mind. For some counselees, the reality of her life can be especially troubling, so help her face reality accompanied by a great hope in God.

If your counselee continues to hallucinate, she should be evaluated by a psychiatrist. Then he or she would decide if the person should be placed on an anti-psychotic medication. Pray and ask God for wisdom. It could be that the counselee is hallucinating due to a lack of sleep or something else may be happening such as schizophrenia. A psychiatrist should be the one to sort that out.

Either way, pray for your counselee that God will give her a sound mind and exhort her to think about things that are true and God-honoring. Also, exhort her to humble herself before God like King Nebuchadnezzar finally did in Daniel, chapter four.

Now I, Nebuchadnezzar, praise, exalt and honor the King of heaven for all His works are true and His ways just, and He is able to humble those who walk in pride (Daniel 4:37).

What if your counselee stays stuck in her characteristics of someone deeply emotionally disturbed? What if you find yourself telling her the same things over and over?

What if She Does Not Make Progress?

She has an overall pattern of an unbelieving heart. Revisit the Gospel even if she has all the correct answers to questions about the Gospel. I would ask her, "Has there ever been a time when you had the desire or asked God to *use* you however He chooses?" Unbelievers usually say "no" to this question and often say, "I will not." I suppose a Christian could recoil at that question, but for the most part, it is a person with an unbelieving heart.

Encourage her to repent. Say something like: "Go to a quiet room and pray and beg God to have mercy on you and grant you repentance. People can be sorry for their sin, but it is not necessarily godly sorrow. Paul wrote about the difference in 2 Corinthians 7:10. **"For the sorrow that is according to the will of God produces a repentance without regret, leading to salvation, but the sorrow of the world produces death."**

If she continues in her sin but insists she is a Christian, bring in two or more witnesses to exhort her to repent. If she does not repent, then take the matter to the pastors and elders of her church. Let them give you guidance regarding whether to continue the counseling or not. They, also, would need to decide whether to proceed with church discipline (see Matthew 18:15-18). Remember that simply doing her counseling homework is not the same thing as Godly sorrow and repentance from God to her.

The question may come up, "Are they demon-possessed?" I do not know. Their thoughts and actions at times are exceedingly wicked and their emotional pain is at times extreme. Whether they are or not, talk to them (not the demons), exhort them to repent, use Scripture which is alive and powerful. Show love and mercy by bringing in other witnesses if they do not repent.

Conclusion

Do not be intimated by a counselee who has the characteristics of one that is deeply emotionally disturbed. I have counseled several women over my years of counseling that fit this description. Almost all of them eventually have done very well, and the Lord has supernaturally changed them. The bad news is they are sinning. The good news is the hope they have in Christ. You must offer His claims to them.

Chapter Five

Counseling Women in Abusive Relationships

Over the thirty years that I have been a biblical counselor, I have, on occasion, counseled a wife who is in an abusive relationship with her husband. Each situation was different, but the wives had several things in common: (1) they were very frightened and embarrassed to come forward and tell what was happening; (2) they somehow felt responsible and protective of their husband's reputation; (3) they were being greatly manipulated and intimidated; (4) sometimes they and/or the children were in physical danger to be battered or even murdered and (5) sadly, as the children got older, they often would begin to treat their mother like their father did.

I remember the first time a wife told me that if she confronted her husband or told anyone what he was doing, he would kill her. That scared me! I was working with Lou Priolo at the time and asked him what to do. I remember him saying, "You cannot guarantee that her husband will not kill her anyway. She needs to seek shelter and take advantage of the resources that God has given to protect her."

For this chapter, I want to cover a brief overview of how a secular expert views and helps the abusive man and his wife. Then we will see a much more detailed view of how the biblical counselor should help the wife.

Secular Expert

Lundy Bancroft wrote an interesting book entitled *Why Does He Do That? Inside the Minds of Angry and Controlling Men*.[15] Bancroft has good insight into the thinking and actions of an abusive man and the protection of the wife or female partner. He has worked with abusive men in groups for years and writes and speaks on the topic.

---

[15] Bancroft, Lundy. *Why Does He Do That? Inside the Minds of Angry and Controlling Men* (New York: Berkley Books) 2002.

Some of Bancroft's counselees are mandated by the courts to attend counseling and some are there because of pressure from family and friends. Bancroft routinely calls the wife to hear her side of the story but does not tell the husband due to protecting her from harm. He also notifies the wife if her husband has made threats against her.

Insightfully, Bancroft does *not* recommend psychology/therapy help for these men. He says that the psychologist simply helps the men justify their abuse because of the man's upbringing or a previous romantic relationship gone wrong. In other words, they have been "wounded" in some way. He also emphasized that the wife will most likely be slow to seek help and be confused and "brain washed" by her husband to think it is her fault. So, he cautions anyone trying to help her to be extra patient with her. That has also been my experience.

Bancroft is very dogmatic about *not* starting out trying to help the man by putting him in marriage counseling. He says it puts the wife in danger. He recommends waiting for the marriage counseling until the husband has made significant progress and sees his wrong thinking. Bancroft also emphasizes that the counselor should believe the wife when she is afraid and if she is, refer her to an abuse hotline. Take the husband's threats seriously. Lundy is not a Christian and does not think that "converting to God" is something that you can trust with these men. Of course, I disagree with him, but it would probably take a *long* time for the husband to rebuild that trust.

Biblical Counseling View

Separate Counseling: As a rule, I require a wife I am counseling to tell her husband. As biblical counselors we cannot be deceptive, but the wife must tell him, not us. *Abuse is the exception to the rule.* Most likely, putting them together would place the wife in harm's way, and you need to protect her privacy. Be cautious and wise. The three greatest predictors of potential harm to his wife are the husband's history of previous strangulation of his wife or someone else, weapons use, or animal abuse. If there is a history of those things, the wife is in extreme danger, especially if she seeks help.[16]

If the husband agrees or is pressured into counseling by the church, his family, or the courts, it needs to be separate counseling and *not* marriage counseling. Biblical counselors are always taught to hear both sides of the story, but abuse is a case where it would put the wife in danger. Chris Moles is a biblical counselor and pastor who has done extensive work with counseling abusive men. He wrote an excellent book, *The Heart of Domestic Abuse: Gospel Solutions for Men Who Use Control and Violence in the Home*.[17] When Chris Moles counsels an abusive man, he requires the wife to have either a biblical counselor or an advocate who can let Chris know if she feels threatened. In addition, the wife needs counseling to help her sort through the issues of her heart. She also needs a lot of hope.

Giving Hope to the Wife

The greatest hope you could give to any wife is the Gospel. It is the **"power of God for salvation to everyone who believes"** (Romans 1:16-17). Other verses that would give her hope are Lamentations 3:21-25; Romans 8:28-29; 1 Corinthians 10:13; Psalm 4:8; Psalm 37.

The husband is acting very wickedly, and Psalm 37 puts his evildoing into perspective. I call this the "fret not" Psalm.

> **Do not fret because of evildoers, be not envious towards wrongdoers. For they will wither quickly like the grass and fade like the green herb. Trust in the LORD and do good; dwell in the land and cultivate faithfulness. Delight yourself in the LORD; and He will give you the desires of your heart. Commit your way to the LORD, trust also in**

---

[16] Telephone conversation with Chris Moles, July 20, 2018. Moles is the author of an excellent book entitled *The Heart of Domestic Abuse: Gospel Solutions for Men Who Use Control and Violence in the Home* (Bemidji, MN: Focus Publishing, 2015).

[17] Moles, Chris. *The Heart of Domestic Abuse: Gospel Solutions for Men Who Use Control and Violence in the Home* (Bemidji, MN: Focus Publishing, 2020).

> **Him, and He will do it. Rest in the LORD and wait patiently for Him; Do not fret because of him who prospers in his way, because of the man who carries out wicked schemes. Cease from anger and forsake wrath; do not fret; it leads only to evildoing..."** (Psalm 37:1-8).

The entire thirty-seventh Psalm is helpful for a wife who has a wicked husband. It would put her life into perspective and give her hope. Encourage her when she feels discouraged to turn to Psalm 37 and reread it.

An additional way to give her hope is for you and her to pray and ask God for wisdom. James is clear:

> **But if any of you lacks wisdom, let him ask of God, who gives to all generously and without reproach, and it will be given to him. But he must ask in faith without any doubting for the one who doubts is like the surf of the sea, driven and tossed by the wind** (James 1:5-6).

Finally, it gives hope to an abused wife to know that you are committed to helping her. So, tell her that. Also, I normally give a wife like this my cell phone number so that she can call or text me anytime. I have found that counselees do not take advantage of having my number, but it is helpful for both of us when she is struggling.

Data Gathering

When you are gathering data, take careful notes including significant quotes. Such as, "My husband threatened to kill me" or "He placed his hands around my neck and began to strangle me." Your notes may be vital to court testimony. Hopefully, it will not come to that, but you never know. Be sure the date you spoke with her is also in your notes.

Be very patient! She is likely confused and frightened, and her thinking may be way off base. Chris Moles says her seeming paralysis in taking appropriate action is akin to PTSD (Post Traumatic Stress Disorder). However, instead of being off the battlefield, the wife is still *in* the battle. Consequently, secular thought is this is *Complex* PTSD. In other words, the wife remains *hyper-vigilant* to try and avoid her husband's abuse.

Often the husband will scream, yell, curse, belittle her, threaten, tell her she is the problem, she is mentally ill, she is not a good Christian or not a Christian at all. If she were, she would be submissive. Often, he will not let her communicate with her family or friends. He may be extremely jealous. He will lie and threaten her either overtly or subtly, but the message is clear. If that is not enough, often the husband will groom the children to be on his side by telling them how much their mother has hurt him.

If the wife calls the police because her husband is doing threatening and dangerous acts, by the time the police show up, the husband is usually calm, and she is often the one who is hysterical. Fortunately, police and judges are more discerning about these situations than in previous years.

Usually the abuse, especially physical abuse, escalates over time. If the wife tries to exhort him to get help, confronts him in some way, seeks shelter, or attempts to get a protection order from the court or a divorce, it is often a very dangerous time for her. An abusive husband will not forgive *anything,* especially if the wife stands up to him even in a kind way. Sometimes drugs and alcohol are involved but not always. Interestingly, when the husband has been confronted by his wife, he may initially agree with her that he needs help, but within hours or a day or two he changes his mind and totally blames her. I have seen that happen, and it is very discouraging for a wife and her counselor.

Confused and Frightened Thinking

Teach your counselee about renewing her mind (Romans 12:1-2) and what kind of thoughts she is to dwell upon (Philippians 4:8). But be patient with her and know you may have to revisit these biblical principles many times before she embraces them as her own. Here are some examples:

Unbiblical Thinking	God-Honoring, Right Thinking
Maybe this is my fault.	What he is doing is not right. It would not matter who he was married to. He would treat them the same way.
What can I do to avoid him getting angry and cursing at me?	I should be kind and give him a blessing instead, but if he gets angry, God will give me grace to bear up under it. (1Corinthians10:13; and 1 Peter 3:8-9)
I do not want to ruin his reputation.	I should not cover up for the deeds of darkness but instead even expose them biblically. (Ephesians 5:11-12)
How can I do something behind the scenes to keep him from reacting?	How can I overcome evil with good? (Romans 12:21)
He punched and choked me, but he did not intend to kill me.	Reality is he could have murdered me. I need to report this to the police and try to protect myself and the children. (Romans 13:1)

Another way she may be confused and frightened are her bitter thoughts towards her husband and/or God. Explain to her that forgiveness and trust are two different things. She must forgive him in her heart but would likely be a fool to trust him. He is responsible to re-earn her trust. If she is angry or bitter towards God, she must repent. If she harbors bitterness, she will *feel* hurt. Scriptures to teach your counselee are Psalm 37, Matthew 18:35, and 1 Corinthians 13:5. The following are some examples of bitter thoughts and how to help her correct them in a God-honoring way.

Bitter Thoughts	Forgiving, God Honoring Thoughts
I hate him.	I will be kind to him because he does not know the Lord and has no capacity to love me as he should. (Luke 6:35-36)
I wish he were dead.	I wish the Lord would save him – granting him repentance and faith. I will pray for him. (Matthew 5:43-45)
I am going to divorce him and take him for all he is worth.	I will seek counsel from my church about the wisest course of action. (Hebrews 13:17)
I will move away with the kids and he will never see them again.	Seeking shelter and hiding may be the wisest thing to do. I will seek counsel and come up with a good safety plan.
How can he want to have sex again after what he just said to me?	I will pray for him to be convicted of his cruelty and selfishness. Lord, help me to show love whether he deserves it or not. This is one way to overcome evil with good. (Romans 12:21; 1 Corinthians 13:4-7)

Another way the wife may be struggling in her thinking is by having despairing thoughts. Question her for suicidal thoughts and/or plans. It is especially important that you give her encouragement and hope.

Despairing Thoughts	Hope in God Thoughts
I cannot take it anymore.	It feels like I cannot take it, but the Lord will help me bear up under this. (1 Corinthians 10:13)
The only way out is for me to kill myself.	Killing myself will only make matters worse. I need to seek shelter. God will help me. (Psalm 46:1)

There is nothing I can do, even God will not help me.	I have "**need of endurance, so that when [I] have done the will of God, [I] may receive what was promised.**" (Hebrews 10:36, adaption mine)
He will never change.	I do not know if he will ever change or not, but I know I can obey the Lord and be faithful no matter what my husband does. With God's help, I can do what is right and not be frightened. (1 Peter 3:6)
My children hate me.	It seems like that now but "if a man's ways are pleasing to the Lord even his enemies will be at peace with him." I can be kind and not speak to the children about their father in a spiteful way but, when appropriate, give them the facts they need to know. (Proverbs 16:7)
There is no hope.	There is hope with the Lord and, meanwhile, if I must suffer, I want it to be for righteousness sake not because I sinned. (Romans 8:16-18)
I will get into trouble because I did not protect the children sooner. I may end up in jail.	Whether I end up in jail or not, I need to try to protect the children now by going to the pastor and the police and telling them the truth. (Ephesians 5:11-13)

Teach Her

Start with telling her that where we need to begin (except of course for her seeking shelter if necessary) is getting the beam out of her own eye. Explain that the Lord wants her to take 100% responsibility for her sin such as her bitterness or anger. Go over Matthew 7:1-5 with her. That is the **"first take the log out of your own eye, and then you will see clearly to take the speck out of your brother's eye"** passage.

Help her redefine what is happening. Use biblical words instead of abuse, personhood, your worth and dignity. Restate what she is telling you such as "being in Christ," "malice," and "evil thoughts, murders, adulteries, false witness, slanders." Do not fuss at her but kindly take her to Scripture to help her sort out how she should think about herself and her husband.

Teach her the ins and outs of biblical submission. The wife is to be submissive to her husband unless her husband is asking her to sin. Emphasize that God is the highest authority not her husband. The bottom line: If a husband is forbidding her to seek godly counsel, or to tell anyone what is happening, he is asking her to sin, and needs to be reproved. We are told in Scripture to **"expose the deeds of darkness"** and to go to our brothers caught in any trespass gently with a motive to restore them (Ephesians 5:11; Galatians 6:1). For much more detail, I recommend chapter fourteen in *The Excellent Wife* book.[18] One word of caution, it may not be safe or wise for a wife to reprove an abusive husband. Let it be *her* judgment call.

She is to fight back biblically to overcome evil with good, which includes thinking rightly and taking advantage of the resources God has given to protect her and the children.

Emergency Plan of Action

Your counselee needs a plan of action to implement when her husband is irate. It is her judgment call. You may be thinking she should have left him a long time ago. Well, don't be too hard on her. Remember, she is frightened and embarrassed. It is extremely scary for her to take action to protect herself and the children.

---

[18] Peace, Martha. *The Excellent Wife* (Bemidji, MN: Focus Publishing, 1995).

Some of the safety tips and plans would be to hide the keys to the car and house where they will be easy to grab in a hurry. Keep your cell phone always charged and gas in the car. Instruct your children to call 911 if they are old enough or to run to a neighbor's house and ask them to call 911. One wife I counseled would routinely hide her husband's guns when he would be working his way up to a rage.

If the husband is out of control or almost out of control, instruct the children with what to do. For instance, tell them, "If I say to you, come with me. Even if your dad is screaming otherwise, quietly come to me and we will walk out the door." In a tense emergency like this, the wife and her children need to know what to do. It will be difficult enough in the moment to think straight, but she will be better prepared if she and the children have a plan in place.

The elders in her church should help come up with a plan of where to go when the father is out of control. Our church has sheltered various wives from time to time either at another church members' home or a motel. The wife knew ahead of time what to do.

While filing criminal charges against the husband, taking out a protection order, a divorce or separate maintenance lawsuit increases her risk to be hurt, especially during the first three months. However, a legal remedy is usually the wisest course of action. Ask God for wisdom and encourage her to implement a wise and robust plan of action. If the children are in danger and the wife will not take steps to protect them, you may need to do that by reporting the abuse to the Family and Children's Services in your community. You have a moral obligation to try and protect the children (Romans 13:1-2).

Conclusion

We need to be wise and discerning when counseling a wife who is in an abusive relationship. She will need an advocate to come to the counseling and hear what you have to say so the advocate can reinforce your counsel during the week. It may be difficult for the wife to tell you the enormity of what is happening, so be very patient and kind to her. If the husband is willing to come to counseling, do not attempt to put them together for counseling in the beginning. If the wife does not want her husband to know she is seeking counsel, find out why. If her husband is abusive or until you can prove otherwise, take her at her word and protect her privacy.

It is scary for you and your counselee, but God will at that time give you grace to bear up under it (1 Corinthians 10:13). Evil doers exist in this world. Sometimes they sit on the front row at church and teach the most popular Sunday School class. Believe the wife and exhort her to do the right thing and honor her Lord.

> **Do not fret because of evildoers... Trust in the LORD and do good...** (Psalm 37:1, 3).

Biblical Counseling in Practice

Chapter Six

Counseling and Correcting Wrong Ways to Think About Biblical Submission

When *The Excellent Wife* book was published in 1995, I knew I had written a somewhat controversial book. My mother said that young women were not going to like it. I pretty much agreed with her. That did not surprise me because the non-Christian world embraces the philosophies of men and our (for the most part) pagan world has embraced a feminist/social justice philosophy of life. What *has* surprised me is the reaction of many Bible-believing fellow Christians who differ not on the issue of submission, but on the issue of the *extent* of the authority of the husband. As a result, I have found myself challenged to make the issue clearer for the Bible-believing Christian world as well as for the individual ladies I counsel.

Every time I think I have heard all the wrong views about biblical submission of a wife to a husband, another one pops up. Thus far, I have listed eleven views, not substantiated by Scripture, and I want to biblically refute all eleven. Before I do that, however, I will briefly review the five biblical principles on submission of a wife. These are covered in much greater detail in *The Excellent Wife* book.

Biblical Principles Concerning a Wife's Submission to Her Husband

Principle 1. **A wife is to be submissive to her husband in all things unless her husband asks her to sin**. Submission is a role God has given the wife, and in no way does it mean she is inferior to her husband or inferior in God's eyes. Submission includes the big *and* small areas of life.

Submission ends when sin begins. Examples of a husband asking his wife to sin are forbidding her to go to church, forbidding her to talk to the children about God, asking or requiring her to participate in immorality/pornography, and forbidding her to reprove him or come forward as a witness because of his sin (Ephesians 5:22-24, Romans 2:11, Galatians 3:28, Philippians 2:5-8, Genesis 2:18, 1 Corinthians 11:9, Acts 5:29).

Principle 2. **A submissive wife is not afraid to do the right thing**. She overcomes her fear by entrusting herself to God, and if she must suffer, it would be for doing what is right. Doing what is right (or righteous) includes the wife not sinning (1 Peter 3:6,17).

Principle 3. **A wife is to be submissive to her husband even if he is not a Christian** (1 Peter 3:1-2).

Principle 4. **A submissive wife does not dishonor the Word of God**. She shows love to God by obeying His Word (Titus 2:3-5; Colossians 3:18; Matthew 22:36-38).

Principle 5. **A wise wife will seek training and counsel on submission from a godly older woman** (Titus 2:3-5).

Now that we reviewed the biblical principles concerning a wife's submission, let's move on to the misperceptions; but don't be surprised at how many people have been influenced by at least one of these misperceptions.

Eleven Wrong Views of Submission

1. The "Mutual Submission Only" View

The "mutual submission only" view is popular in many churches, but liberal churches typically misuse it to undo submission. Liberal churches are those who do *not* believe the Scriptures are God's Word without error. This view fits nicely with the unbelieving world and the feminist philosophy. Some who hold this view would also say that Paul was a chauvinist and a victim of the Roman culture of his day. However, if you study Paul's writings carefully, you find that Paul backs up his teaching with God's original intent and not the practices of the Roman culture. They also assume that if you hold to a Bible believing view that you think that men are better than, and more

Counseling and Correcting Wrong Ways to Think About Biblical Submission

valuable than, women. The liberal view is also the politically correct view.

Counter it by explaining the context of Ephesians, chapters five and six. Paul wrote, **"...and be subject to one another in the fear of Christ"** (Ephesians 5:21). The "mutual submission only" adherents use that verse to prove their point. However, it is taken out of the context of that passage. Paul was giving a big picture overview to Christians regarding mutual submission. But you must keep reading as he gives several very specific examples under the over-arching umbrella of submission: **"Wives be subject to your own husbands ... Children, obey your parents in the Lord, for this is right ... and Slaves, be obedient to those who are your masters according to the flesh..."** (Ephesians 5:22, 6:1, 6:5).

The mutual submission overview and specific examples are both true. It is not an either/or situation. *All* Christians are to be mutually submissive to each other in a general sense of working together in humility, harmony, and love. *Some* Christians have additional obligations concerning submission such as the wife to her husband or child to his parent.

2. <u>The Pastor's View</u>

This would account for the fact that so many Christian ladies have never heard of the Bible's teaching on submission. It seems that this is the view of most Bible-believing pastors. Likely, they know that the Bible's teaching regarding biblical submission of a wife to her husband is true and right, but they rationalize not teaching it because it might downsize their church considerably.

On the rare occasion when I have an opportunity to talk with a pastor who holds to this view, I encourage him to help his ladies by lovingly teaching this doctrine from the pulpit. One pastor did that and later told me that within his sermon he played a section of one of my recordings explaining submission. He said, "That way, it was *you* telling them and not *me.*" I laughed and thought, "That is the only sermon I will ever preach!"

3. The "I'm Submissive, I Would Never Sell the House without My Husband's permission" View

It makes me wonder if she could not sell the house because her husband's name is on the deed. Many wives believe themselves to be submissive because they would never "cross" their husbands when it comes to big issues, such as selling the house, buying a car, or having another baby. However, if you talked with their husbands, many would say, "She fights me every step of the way over big issues as well as small."

To help the wife understand, illustrate with the example of a child obeying a parent. Should the child obey only if it is really important? Of course, it is not all right for the one under authority to decide what is important. The child is to obey unless Providentially hindered, asked to sin against God, or unless the child makes an appeal, and the parent changes their mind.

The best illustration is the example of obedience to God. Are Christians to obey God in large *and* small matters *or* are they to obey God based on what *seems* to be especially important to them? Of course, God requires and expects all levels of obedience.

> **As obedient children, do not be conformed to the former lusts which were yours in your ignorance, but like the Holy One who called you, be holy yourselves also in all your behavior: because it is written, "You shall be holy, for I am holy"** (1 Peter 1:14-15).

Exhort her to be faithful in the small things as well as the large. Show her the words of our Lord.

> **He who is faithful in a very little thing is faithful also in much; and he who is unrighteous in a very little thing is unrighteous also in much** (Luke 16:10).

Explain that submission is a heart's attitude as well as an outward action. If her motive is right (to show love to God *and* to her husband), the wife will consider even the small issues to be of paramount importance to God and to her husband.

> **Let love be without hypocrisy. Abhor what is evil; cling to what is good. Be devoted to one another in brotherly love; give preference to one another in honor...** (Romans 12:9-10).

Submission should be from the husband's perspective and not from the perspective of what the wife thinks is important. The "spirit of the matter" includes the husband's desires or preferences, not just the times when he gives an absolute order or dictate. For example, when a husband says, "Honey I think I prefer to not have so much starch in the collar of my shirts" compared to "Do not put starch in my collar." The wife should want so much to please her husband and show love to him and to maintain the spirit of submission that she should be faithful in the least. Exhort her to consider even the least requests and opinions of her husband as possibly a submission issue and therefore important. That is seeing submission from his perspective and being faithful in the least little things.

4. The "I Can't Take it Anymore and God Understands" View

This sort of thinking comes from a bitter heart. The wife has been hurt and she is likely playing those hurts over and over in her mind. Her emotional pain becomes greater and greater. God is further and further away from her thoughts, or God may be in her thoughts but in the wrong way. For instance, "Why doesn't God help me with this?"

She needs hope such as from 1 Corinthians 10:13, Romans 8:28-29, and Lamentations 3:21-25. Simply tell her that it is *not true* that she "can't take it anymore, even though it does feel like it." What *is true* is that **"God is faithful and will not allow her to be pressured beyond what she is able to bear"** (1 Corinthians 10:13). Have her read Jay Adams' *Christ and Your Problems* booklet.[19] Also have her complete Lou Priolo's *Bitterness* study.[20]

---

[19] Adams, Jay. *Christ and Your Problems* (Phillipsburg, NJ, 1999).
[20] Priolo, Lou. *Bitterness* (Phillipsburg, NJ, 2008).

Exhort her to forgive her husband (Ephesians 4:31-32), work at overcoming evil with good (Romans 12:21) and give her husband blessings instead (1 Peter 3:9). Also exhort her to put on love to her husband. For example, "Love does not take into account a wrong suffered. Instead of sitting here thinking about what he has done to me, I am going to take this time to think of something nice I can do for him and then I am going to do it." Or "I'm going to take this time and energy to pray for my husband and ask the Lord how I can help my husband."

Explain to her that she has a wrong view of God if she thinks that "God understands that I can't take it." God requires that she forgive in her heart whether her husband ever changes or not. Be sure and tell her that forgiveness and trust are two different things. Christians not only must forgive, but also be discerning. Sometimes a wife would be a fool to trust her husband after something he has done. He is the one who must rebuild her trust over time. It would be easy for a wife to be bitter when her husband has sinned against her. Instead, she is to turn to the Lord and forgive her husband in her heart. God will help her.

5. The "Obey Even if He Asks You to Sin" View

This is an immensely wrong view. We are not to sin against God. Teach her the biblical view of authority. **"For there is no authority except from God, and those which exist are established by God"** (Romans 13:1, 1 Corinthians 11:3, Matthew 28:18). God is the highest authority, and He is the one who ordains and limits all other lesser authorities such as kings or queens, husbands, parents, or slave owners.

God is holy and cannot tempt anyone to sin (James 1:13-14). Men are sinful and do, at times, tempt or even command others to sin. However, God has provided several "means of grace" for the Christian to respond when ordered to sin by someone in authority over them. Those "means of grace" are the grace of the indwelling Holy Spirit, the Scriptures, and other brothers and sisters in the Lord helping to "bear their burdens" (Galatians 6:2).

The Lord has also provided other resources to protect a wife whose husband is asking her to sin, mainly, church discipline if her husband is a Christian (Matthew 18:15-18) and the governing authorities in whatever country they live in. There may be times that the Lord gives a wife an opportunity to suffer for righteousness sake (1 Peter 4:14-16,19). For example, if a wife refuses to participate in a sinful sex act with her husband. He may pout or threaten to divorce her or scream at her in a rage. If her motives are pure before the Lord and she is respectful and otherwise submissive to her husband, she will be suffering for righteousness sake.

Be prepared to refute the misunderstanding that Sarah is praised in Scripture because she obeyed Abraham by lying for him when she said, "I am his sister." The deception was that she was *not* his wife. Sarah *was* his half-sister, but she deliberately deceived the king because Abraham was afraid he would be killed because his wife was so beautiful.

Explain that stories in the Old Testament (narratives) are just that – stories. They are true and point to what God is doing, but they were never intended for us to follow personally everything we read about. Nowhere does Peter praise Sarah specifically because Sarah lied for Abraham.

> **For in this way in former times the holy women also, who hoped in God, used to adorn themselves, being submissive to their own husbands; just as Sarah obeyed Abraham, calling him lord, and you have become her children if you do what is right without being frightened by any fear** (1 Peter 3:5-6).

The context of Peter's letter is suffering. Within the context of suffering for the Lord's sake, women married to unbelievers as well as believers will sometimes suffer. If she is a godly woman then her true adornment will show her gentle and quiet spirit and submission to her husband. Peter does not refer to Sarah's lying as "doing what is right." He does *not* mention the lying incident. He *does* refer to her being submissive to her husband. In other words, as a pattern in Sarah's life she was submissive to her husband.

I think a good illustration would be King David. As a pattern in his life, he had a heart for God, yet we know there were some things about his life that we are not to copy, such as the adultery with Bathsheba. Narrative stories have legitimate points, such as seeing God's providential care or His justice or His mercy. Think of the book of Esther. Esther did a lot of things that God providentially used for His glory and His purposes, but there is much in what she did that Christian women today are not to copy.

For example, Esther did not tell the king or anyone in the king's palace or harem that she was a Jew, yet the Old Testament specifically forbids mixed marriages outside of their faith (Esther 2:10). The fact that Moredecai (her cousin who was her guardian) told her not to tell her nationality still does not make it right. Mordecai should not have asked her, and Esther should have appealed to him to get out of trying out for the king's harem. The point of the story was *God and His faithfulness to keep His promises.* The point was not to find your daughter a husband in such a way or for her to be deceptive. God obviously uses people in spite of their sin.

So, Peter is saying to do what is right, be submissive to your husband and have a right heart attitude. That is all he is saying, and we should not read more into it than God and Peter intended. Teach her a right view of suffering. It is a privilege to suffer for the Lord's sake and for truly doing what is right. It is foolish to suffer unnecessarily. Unnecessary suffering is like shooting yourself deliberately in the foot and expect to be praised for how terrible it is to suffer in that way. A wife should not suffer for being rebellious or disrespectful, but if her husband asks her to sin and she suffers for appealing and, if necessary, for refusing, then she is honoring God.

As a counselor you need to be aware that many Christian women's books dogmatically teach the "obey even if he asks you to sin" view. In Darien Cooper's book, *You Can Be the Wife of a Happy Husband*, she wrote, "God has outlined in His Word the fact that He wants her to obey her husband *without exception.*"[21] It is dangerous to take that view because some husbands do sin and try to intimidate their wives into participating in the sin with them. Husbands are not the highest authority, God is. So, if her husband is asking or demanding that she sin, she must obey God.

---

[21] Cooper, Darien. *You Can be the Wife of a Happy Husband* (Colorado Springs, CO: Chariot Victor Publishing, 1976).

Counseling and Correcting Wrong Ways to Think About Biblical Submission

6. The View that Nowhere in the Bible does it say a Wife Can Reprove her Husband.

Well, nowhere in the Bible does it *not* say for a wife to reprove her husband. The Bible *does* say for the wife to be respectful (Ephesians 5:33); to have a gentle and quiet spirit (1 Peter 3:4); to be under her husband's authority (Ephesians 5:22); and to love her husband (Titus 2:4). These *specific* mandates apply to a wife but so do all the other mandates regarding conflict solving biblically and dealing with other people's sin. One word of caution is to warn the wife that her tone should be extra respectful and kind when reproving her husband but speak the truth in love.

The Bible often instructs us in areas that apply to all Christians. Every possible contingency is not spelled out. Often, we are left to make the appropriate application. In addition to specific mandates, there are general mandates for every Christian such as **"overcome evil with good," "bear one another's burdens," "if your brother sins, go to him privately,"** and **"put off anger and put on kindness"** (Romans 12:21; Galatians 6:2; Matthew 18:15; Ephesians 4:29-31). Very often counselees are confused about this issue, and you will need to carefully teach her and pray that God will give her grace to understand and apply these principles in her life with her husband.

Along with this teaching is the view about how much a wife should protect a husband who is sinning.

7. The "I will Come Forward as a Witness only if My Husband Commits Adultery, Sexually Molests the Children, or Commits Murder" View

This is a common misconception regarding biblical submission. Elizabeth Handford in her book, *Me Obey Him?* wrote "God did not make a woman her husband's judge. He is accountable to God for his own decision, his own behavior, his own sin."[22]

---

[22] Handford, Elizabeth. *Me Obey Him?* (Murfreesboro, TN: Sword of the Lord Publishers, 1972).

I agree that the husband is accountable to God, but God *did* make a wife her husband's judge in the sense that she is to make righteous, godly, objective judgments. She is not to make self-righteous, pharisaical, judging motives judgments. She is to make judgments concerning outward statements and behavior. It is wrong to scream at the children in anger. It is wrong for a husband to bully his wife through sinful intimidation. These are judgments that all Christians are to make and (if appropriate) to act upon.

Sin is sin and whether you are talking about anger, lust, murder, or adultery, God has given clear instructions with what to do when someone sins against you. I do not believe we are to arbitrarily choose which sins we consider the greater sins, which are the lesser sins, and which ones are optional to obey or not when reproving sin. Certainly, some sins are of such magnitude that they must be dealt with very quickly while others can be dealt with more patiently, but a wife is still to come forward as a witness to try to help her husband if he will not turn from his sin.

8. The "Win Him Without a Word" View

This view is often espoused with the previous one, "obey even if he asks you to sin" view. The "win him without a word view" is the basis for some teaching that a wife is not to reprove her husband or come forward as a witness against him, even if he is in unrepentant sin. Instead, she is to not say anything and thus, "win him without a word." This wrong view is based on a wrong understanding of 1 Peter 3:1-2.

> **In the same way, you wives, be submissive to your own husbands so that even if any of them are disobedient to the word, they may be won without a word by the behavior of their wives, as they observe your chaste and respectful behavior** (1 Peter 3:1-2).

Two key phrases to understand are **"disobedient to the word"** and **"may be won without a word."** Peter plainly defines those who are **"disobedient to the word,"** and that is a phrase that describes unbelievers. In a few verses before 1 Peter 3, Peter clearly defines those who are disobedient to God's Word as those who reject the Cornerstone (Jesus), and they stumble and are offended by Him. **"... for they stumble because they are disobedient to the word and to this doom they were also appointed"** (1 Peter 2:6-9).

Peter's point is not about reproof (telling the husband what he is doing wrong) but about sharing the Gospel with an unsaved husband. The wife is to actively evangelize him by her chaste and respectful behavior and her godly heart attitudes, not by preaching to him and stuffing Gospel tracts under his pillow. In other words, she is not to be a hypocritical Christian who professes Christ and treats her husband in a disrespectful way.

There are other general commands to all Christians, and they also apply to husbands and wives whom, if they are both Christians, are brothers and sisters in the Lord. They are to help each other become as much like the Lord as possible; gently reproving each other in love, with a motive to restore the other person (Galatians 6:1).

If the husband is an unbeliever, there are general commands of how to deal with unbelievers who are acting foolishly such as **"Do not answer a fool according to his folly..."** (Proverbs 26:4-5). Scripture also tells us to appeal to an unbeliever's conscience to do what is right. Keep in mind that wives are to be helpers-suitable to their husbands. All husbands and wives have sinful weaknesses, and it is understood from Scripture that "gently and lovingly" they are to try to help each other. Jesus said in Matthew 22:39, **"Love your neighbor ..."** Her husband is her closest neighbor.

9. <u>The "I Don't Have to Obey because He is Not a Christian" View</u> (This is common.)

This thinking is clearly refuted in 1 Peter 3:1-2 which says, **"Be submissive to your own husbands so that even if any of them are disobedient to the word ..."** (1 Peter 3:1-2). We have already seen in this chapter that those who are "disobedient to the word" are defined by Peter as unbelievers who reject Christ.

When counseling a wife who holds to this misperception, assume her motive is good but that she is ignorant of what the Bible really teaches. If ignorance is not the problem, then she is likely rebellious.

10. The Husband's View

Some husband's demand that their wives not tell anyone what they have done wrong. Often, this is sinful intimidation/manipulation on the part of the husband. He is asking his wife to go against Scripture and cover up for him. Sometimes it *is* necessary for her to come forward as a witness to protect others and try to help her husband. If he is a Christian (or says he is) then it is the responsibility of the church to judge those within the church (Matthew 18:15-18, 1 Corinthians 5:9-13).

It is ultimately unfair and frustrating for her pastor if the wife has given him vague hints in the past but was unclear about the situation. Subsequently, she is hurt and angry at her pastor because he did not follow through. Anyone who comes forward as a witness needs to be crystal clear with specific examples. It would be like a patient going to her doctor and saying, "Well I'm mostly okay, but I don't feel the best today." Instead of saying, "I am having crushing chest pain and think I am having a heart attack."

The wife or family may be the only ones to know, since many people put on a good front in public and at church. For example, I once counseled a wife whose husband was a pillar in their church. He was a deacon, taught the adult Sunday School class, and was a well-known businessman in his community. At home, he was a tyrant with an extreme anger problem. He bullied his wife and children, and they were never to "tell." Unfortunately, the wife did not even know to come forward as a witness or start the church discipline process because her church virtually ignored the Scriptures about church discipline. I counseled her, showed her in the Scriptures, and exhorted her to take it as far as the church would allow. Churches like that would probably not follow up with the third step of church discipline: **"tell it to the church"** (Matthew 18:17). The pastors would not only *not* tell it to the church but also might not even try to help her husband. It is difficult to counsel a godly wife whose church will not do the right thing. But again, she should take it as far as the church would allow.

It is understandable why a wife who has been threatened or intimidated would say nothing. However, she runs the risk of disobeying God by not coming forward as a witness; and she also runs a risk of becoming so embittered that she compounds her husband's sin by leaving him or unbiblically divorcing him.

11. A Husband Threatening to Divorce his Wife if She Does Not Submit.

Certainly, this threat is always wrong, but as her counselor, do make sure that what the wife is refusing to do is sinful on her part. For example, it is a sin to knowingly sign a joint income tax statement that has false information. It is not a sin to go out to eat in a restaurant that serves alcohol if the husband is not requiring her to get drunk.

This kind of threat from the husband is intimation and manipulation. Often, he makes threats if she will not cover up for his sin or if she refused to participate in sinful sexual acts. Instruct her to say something like, "It would be terribly difficult for me if you divorce me. That is not right and that is not what I want. But, if you do, God will give me grace to go through it" (based on 1 Corinthians 10:13).

Just when I thought I had heard all the wrong views out there, this one popped up – "Complementarianism positions a wife to be abused." Those that adhere to complementarianism, as I do, believe that the wife is to be a complement (not a compliment) to her husband. She helps him, completes him, and fulfills the godly role that God ordained for her.

Being in God's will includes taking full advantage of the biblical resources that God has provided for a wife to be protected. In the case of abuse, one of those resources that might become necessary is to call the police and report what her husband is doing (Romans 13:1-2). It is not ever God's design for the family or the Bible's teachings that are the problem. Whenever there is abuse someone sinfully distorted

God's design. For more information on this wrong view, see the next chapter in this book, "Counseling Women Who Long to be Equal."

Conclusion

If we are honest, nobody really likes being told what to do, but as Christians it should be our joy and not a burden to obey God when it comes to being submissive to those in God-given authority over us. It is no wonder that there are so many misperceptions concerning the issue of biblical submission and new ones pop up on occasion. As you counsel, study the issue of submission; and, thus, be prepared to refute any misperception that your counselee may have.

Chapter Seven

Counseling Women Who Desire to be Equal

I grew up in a traditional conservative home. My parents were married and faithful to each other. My dad worked and my mother stayed home. She was a wonderful housewife, cook, and mother. We lived in a small house near Atlanta, and I attended public schools. None of us were Christians, but we had conservative ethics. I was very shielded from most of the outside world. I had never heard of homosexuality until I was in my high school years.

During those years, the political winds began to have great influence over people's thinking. They appealed to the love of the world. The Apostle John warned about worldliness in his letter entitled 1 John.

> **Do not love the world nor the things in the world. If anyone loves the world, the love of the Father is not in him. For all that is in the world, the lust of the flesh and the lust of the eyes and the boastful pride of life, is not from the Father, but is from the world. The world is passing away, and also its lusts; but the one who does the will of God lives forever** (1 John 2:15-17).

In the 1960's, I graduated from high school and college, got married, and had a baby. They were the years of the Playboy philosophy and the sexual revolution. Betty Friedan wrote her ground-breaking book, *The Feminine Mystique,* and formed The National Association of Women with Muriel Fox in 1966, which started the modern feminist movement. Women had their ears tickled because, after all, they did not want to be (as Friedan wrote) a "non-person." Friedan's thought was that women's mental development had been arrested at an infantile level, short of personal identity. They loudly demanded equality in everything—education, pay, marriage, and ultimately equal rights in the church to be pastors, preachers, and teachers of men. Political rhetoric can fan the winds of discontent, but it can also be found within our own hearts.

Our sinful hearts long to have their own way. Another idea coming to the forefront, even among Bible believing Christians today, is the idea that if a woman is biblically submissive to her husband, she positions herself to be abused. Consequently, those who are influenced by the feminist movement are enticed by their own sinful hearts to struggle against God's design for them in the home and in the church, and wrongly think about the issue of submission and abuse.

Because of this, I would like to define biblical complementarianism and explain how it affects the role of men and women in the church and in the home. Also, I will address my concerns about how the political winds are wrongly affecting some Bible believing Christians and how the issue of abuse in the home and church plays into this topic. This chapter concludes with practical application for biblical counseling.

Complementarianism and the Role of Husbands and Wives

Complementarianism (think complete not compliment) is the role that God has given husbands and wives in marriage. The husband is to be the leader and the wife is to be his suitable helper. This was and is God's plan from the beginning of creation. The Apostle Paul explains it in 1 Corinthians 11:8-9.

> **For man does not originate from woman, but woman from man; for indeed man was not created for the woman's sake, but woman for the man's sake.**

I tell my counselees that men need *help* and that is why God created Eve. This is not an afterthought or first century male bias of the Apostle Paul for the wife to be content in her biblical role. It harkens back to God's original intent.

Those who deny what the Bible teaches about submission of the wife are called egalitarians. In other words, the wife is equal in authority to her husband and women church members are in equal authority with the pastors. It would be very difficult, if not impossible, for a wife who adheres to egalitarianism to be joyful and content in her role in the home and in the church.

Counseling Women Who Desire to be Equal

It is important to learn the biblical principles regarding a wife's submission and role in the home. I will not take time now to go over those principles, but they are explained in detail in *The Excellent Wife* book. Scripture is clear that submission does not mean the wife is to be a robot or a doormat who never has an opinion. How could she possibly help her husband if she does not have good opinions? However, she needs to not set her heart on having her way. That is where the problems and conflicts arise.

In Philippians 2, we are told that Jesus submitted Himself to the Father, **"... who, although He existed in the form of God, did not regard equality with God a thing to be grasped, but emptied Himself... He humbled Himself by becoming obedient to the point of death..."** (Philippians 2:6-8). Certainly, He was not inferior to God the Father. He took on that role to carry out the glorious plan of redemption. Likewise, neither are wives inferior to their husbands. In fact, they may be superior in some ways—perhaps smarter, better educated, etc. Scripture tells us clearly that **"... there is no partiality with God"** in the context of referring to the salvation of men, women, Jews, or Gentiles (Romans 2:11). In Galatians 3:28, the Apostle Paul explained **"that there is neither Jew nor Greek, there is neither slave nor free man, there is neither male nor female; for you are all one in Christ Jesus."**

What about the woman's role in the church? Scripture teaches that only men are to be elders or pastors. The pastoral epistles (1 and 2 Timothy and Titus) explain the qualifications of one aspiring to be a pastor. Obviously, they are men. There is no wiggle room for women to fit into these descriptions, such as **"*husband* of one wife"** and **"one who manages his own household well"** (1 Timothy 3:2,4). Likewise, deacons must be **"men of dignity"** and **"these men must first be tested..."** (1 Timothy 3:8, 10). All three pastoral epistles describe the elder/pastor/deacon qualifications as belonging to men, not women.

Women are to use their spiritual gifts and talents in the church under their husband's and elders' authority. They are not to be teaching the men in the church. 1 Timothy 3 tells us **"but I do not allow a woman to teach or exercise authority over a man"** in the context of the church. But note, there *is* a special place for the godly older woman to teach the younger women. See Titus 2:3-5. There are also women no matter their age who have the gift of teaching. They should be using that gift teaching other women and children.

What Submission is and is Not

Again, submission is *not* being a doormat and *never* having an opinion. It is not outwardly obeying but resenting it in your heart. It also is not only being submissive with the big issues, such as selling your house, or within the church, agreeing that only men should be elders.

Submission is not unbiblically covering up for your husband's or elder's sin. In marriage, submission is not arguing or pouting or giving your husband the cold shoulder until he gives in. Then saying, "My husband said I could do this!" Lastly, submission does not mean obeying when a husband asks his wife to sin. Understanding that God is the highest authority, a wife must respectfully decline.

Submission in the home and the church is not a burden but is considered by the wife to be her joy to honor God, her husband, and her elders. She holds to the Scripture **"For this is the love of God, that we keep His commandments; and His commandments are not burdensome"** (1 John 5:3). In cases where her husband cannot be reached for his opinion, a godly wife will make decisions based on what she thought her husband would do. That is the "spirit of the law," and a wife like that has a heart for God.

Biblical submission is a way for the wife to show love to God (by obeying Him) and love to her husband and elders (by not seeking her own way) (Matthew 22:35-40; 1 Corinthians 13:5). It is a mark of a woman who has a gentle and quiet spirit. She is precious in God's sight. She accepts God's dealings with her as good and is not given to anger or fear (see 1 Peter 3:3-6).

How not being submissive affects the home and the church.

First, a woman who is rebellious is not being a joy to her husband or her pastors if she is resenting submission outwardly or in her heart (Hebrews 13:17). It is especially troubling to think that if she comes to the communion table with unconfessed sin in her heart, she is coming in an unworthy manner (1 Corinthians 11:23-31). Also, more than likely in her home, her husband and children will be aware of her resentment. Thus, they will view her as a counterfeit Christian on Sundays when she is at church or participating in devotions with the family at home. Instead, her love for God is to be **"...without hypocrisy"** [pretending] (Romans 12:9, explanation mine).

Worse than her family or church leaders knowing she resents being submissive, God will know she is struggling and that it is not her joy to live out the plan He has for her. She is leaning on her own understanding and thus being wise in her own eyes. Exhort her with the following Scriptures:

> **Trust in the Lord with all your heart and do not lean on your own understanding** (Proverbs 3:5).
>
> **How blessed are those whose way is blameless, who walk in the law of the LORD. How blessed are those who observe His testimonies, who seek Him with all their heart...** [they think] **Your testimonies also are my delight; they are my counselors** (Psalm 119:1-2,24, explanation mine).

The influence of the political winds

Unfortunately, the political winds of today are influencing even Bible believing Christians who say they are complementarians. The "winds" of today are the Feminist Movement and being "woke" to their rights. One way this is shown is by Bible believing Christians who link abuse with biblical submission. In other words, some are saying that being submissive positions a wife to be abused. Abuse (the husband's sin) is a separate issue and should be dealt with biblically and legally. It is the husband's sinful bent that causes him to treat his wife in a sinful/abusive way. It is not because she is being a godly wife.

If the husband is sinning by acting like a fool or being harsh with her or (in the extreme) pushing, hitting, or threatening to do so, she should be wise and seek shelter and/or help from the elders in her church. To not do so would be unbiblically and possibly unlawfully covering up for him. If he professes to be a Christian and is unrepentant, then church discipline is appropriate. Also, pressing legal charges against him would likely be appropriate. If he is not a Christian, then the best avenue would be for her to ask his family and friends to help her with an intervention and/or pursue legal charges (see Matthew 18:15-18; Romans 13:1-2).

Even Bible believing Christians are influenced by the "woke" political culture and seem to not tolerate Christian wives whose joy it is to serve their husband and their Lord by being biblically submissive. For those whom it is their joy, they are submissive not only in the "big" things but also the "little."

Your counselee may have been influenced by Christian women authors who give mixed messages to others about submission in their speaking, writing, and social media connections. In other words, they say they believe they should be submissive to their husbands and church leaders, but they obviously struggle with the concept. Some even blame the Apostle Paul's writings in the Bible for the woman's plight. They ignore the fact that what Paul wrote is just as God-breathed as the words of Jesus in the Gospels.

> [Paul wrote] **For this reason we also constantly thank God that when you received the word of God which you heard from us, you accepted it not as the word of men, but for what it really is, the word of God, which also performs its work in you who believe** (1 Thessalonians 2:13).

Counseling Women Who Desire to be Equal

Bringing it all together

The following bullet points are important for the counselor to teach and exhort the counselee regarding the influence of the feminist movement and her own sinful heart. Teach her and exhort her to think clearly about this subject.

- A wife should gratefully accept God's role for her and see it as a privilege to be a true "helper-suitable" to her husband. God's original intent has not changed (see 1 Corinthians 11:1-3, 8-9).

- She should be a joy for her elders in her church and graciously submit to their authority thus contributing to order and reverence in worship in the church. When we worship, our audience is God; and we want Him to be pleased (see Hebrews 13:17).

- We all need to follow the Scriptures and not the world's opinions that tickle our ears (see 2 Timothy 4:3-4).

- A godly Christian wife loves the Lord with all her heart and sees God's sovereign rule over her as good for her. It is God's perfect plan. She looks to the Scriptures to obey them with all her heart (see Matthew 22:37-40)

- She takes seriously the biblical mandates to follow, if necessary, the biblical resources to protect herself and the children when her husband is sinning. For example, **"...do not answer a fool according to his folly"** (Proverbs 26:4-5), or the steps of church discipline (Matthew 18:15-18) or notifying the police (Romans 13:1-2).

- She has a gentle and quiet spirit and thus accepts God's dealings with her as good and is not given to anger or fear (1 Peter 3:3-6).

Conclusion

Political winds come and go. Some blow harder than others as they influence the Christian world. Our responsibility as counselors is to recognize their influence and help our counselees to become discerning. Help them have joy in honoring God as they fulfill their role that God has intended for them.

Chapter Eight

Counseling Women Who are Depressed

Debbie comes to see you because she needs help. She has on no makeup and her hair has not been washed. You notice dark circles under her eyes. She is frequently sighing and there are tears in her eyes. When you ask her "what's wrong?" she says, "I often feel sad and unhappy, but lately it has been far worse than usual. I can't eat. I can't sleep very well. I do not want to be around anyone. When my husband goes to work and the kids are in school, I go back to bed and just lie there. I feel guilty because my husband must go to the store for me, and he does the cooking and takes care of the kids. My mother comes over and helps clean and wash clothes and iron. There are days that I simply wish I were dead. I have prayed and asked God to help me, but I am only getting worse. I don't know what to do. Can you help me?"

Obviously, Debbie needs a lot of help. She is in a very precarious place emotionally and as her counselor, you need to know what to do. This chapter will tell you how to gather data, give hope (a lot of hope!), what basic biblical principles you need to teach her, and very practical applications using the Scriptures as the basis.

Gathering Data

When I was trained as a biblical counselor under Lou Priolo and Howard Eyrich, they taught me that depression is almost always more than one issue. Sometimes it is not always obvious, and as a result you should not forget to weep with those who weep. Be patient with a counselee going through a season of depression, God may simply be testing them; but start by gathering data. The easiest way to find out is to ask questions and go over the four major contributing causes with your counselee. The four major causes are circumstances, physical problems, bitterness, and sin. Bitterness is, of course, a sin but it is separated out in this list because it is a huge contributing factor.

Biblical Counseling in Practice

The following is a list of examples of what you need to ask your counselee. As I am talking to her, I also am writing on the white board in my office the list of four factors and what she tells me about each one. When we are finished, it is obvious to both of us what is likely causing her depression – not just one thing but a combination of things. I will tell her that most of the problems on the list are things that can be changed with God's help. What cannot be changed, He will help her to think and respond rightly and give her grace to bear up under it. Here are some examples:

1. <u>Circumstances</u>

> Past or present trauma, death of a loved one, financial difficulties, some sort of trial, a difficult marriage. She may think of something else that needs to be added.

2. <u>Physical</u>

> Physical exhaustion, illness, sleep loss, reaction to medications, poor diet, vitamin deficiency, anemia, hypoglycemia, hypothyroidism, chronic illness, and pain.

3. <u>Bitterness</u>

> When questioning her about bitterness ask, "In your life, who has hurt you the most?" She may say, "no one." Or she may think of a whole list of people. If so, write down the names.

4. <u>Sin</u>

> Guilt over sin can cause depression (Psalm 32:1-5). Three *huge* contributing sin factors are self-pity, worry, and vain regrets. If she does not mention those, ask her, "Do you have a tendency to feel sorry for yourself?" "Are you a worrier?" "Do you think about things that happened in the past that you regret?" Depending on the counselee, I would probably ask her, "Have you ever had an abortion?" Other sins she might mention could

be gluttony, irresponsibility, anger, lying, immorality, envy, stealing, deceitfulness, rebellion, complaining, selfishness, vanity, and lust.

Once you have completed gathering this phase of the data, you can explain to your counselee that it is a combination of things. Then give her hope that for the items on the list that she, with God's help, can change. Tell her that you will help her with them. Also, tell her that for the things that cannot be changed, such as death of a loved one, God can comfort her and give her grace to think rightly about it. An example would be, "God thank you for the years I did have my mother. Thank you for reminding me how much I need you."

Giving Hope

Without a doubt the greatest hope that you could ever give your counselee is the Gospel. The Gospel is not only her greatest hope but also her only hope. Question her about her salvation. I really think it is especially telling if you ask the diagnostic evangelism question, "If you died today and stood before the Lord and He said, 'Why should I let you into My heaven?' What would you say?" It is common for me to hear either a fuzzy answer, such as, "I asked Jesus into my heart when I was six years old," or a works centered answer: "I tried really hard and hope I have been good enough." Even if she gives an accurate answer, revisit the Gospel with her either in one of the first counseling sessions or for homework.[23]

Other verses on hope are 1 Corinthians 10:13; Matthew 11:28-30; Romans 8:28-30; Romans 5:1-5; and Psalms 8, 16, 19, 119. Give her "hope" verses for homework and tell her if she has trouble concentrating to stand up and read them aloud. She may need to read the same verse several times and ask God to help her comprehend them. You want to point her upward to God and away from her self-focus.

---

[23] Peace, Martha. *The Excellent Wife* (Bemidji, MN: Focus Publishing, 1995).

Teach her Scriptural Examples.

When counseling someone who is depressed, I always teach them the following biblical examples: The Psalmist in Psalm 42, Jeremiah in Lamentations chapter 3, and the Apostle Paul in 2 Corinthians 4:8-18. I begin with the Psalmist and explain how his thinking vacillated between his tears and his hope in God.

> **As the deer pants for the water brooks, so my soul pants for You, O God. My soul thirsts for God, for the living God; when shall I come and appear before God? My tears have been my food day and night... Why are you in despair, O my soul? And why have you become disturbed within me? Hope in God, for I shall again praise Him for the help of His presence...** (Psalm 42:1-3, 5).

Next, I move on to Lamentations 3:1-25. I give a brief context of the book of Lamentations and tell who Jeremiah was. I instruct her to tell me after each one of the first 20 verses if she feels the way Jeremiah did – yes or no. Often, my counselee feels the way Jeremiah did. Here is a sampling from the first twenty verses in Lamentations chapter three.

> **I am the man who has seen affliction because of the rod of His [God's] wrath... Surely against me He has turned His hand repeatedly all the day... In dark places He has made me dwell, like those who have long been dead... even when I cry out and call for help, He shuts out my prayer... My soul has been rejected from peace; I have forgotten happiness. So I say, "My strength has perished, and so has my hope from the LORD"** (Lamentations 3:1, 3, 6, 8, 17-18).

Before verse 21, I stop and say, "Jeremiah's circumstances never got any better, but most likely yours will. However, even in the midst of despair, he remembered something and hope flooded back into his heart."

> **This I recall to mind, therefore I have hope. The LORD's lovingkindnesses indeed never cease, for His compassions never fail. They are new every morning; Great is Your faithfulness. "The LORD is my portion," says my soul, "Therefore I have hope in Him." The LORD is good to those who wait for Him, to the person who seeks Him** (Lamentations 3:21-25).

Jeremiah turned *from* lamenting *to* thinking rightly about God *to* bursting into praise for Him!

My last example is the Apostle Paul in 2 Corinthians. Tell your counselee that Paul went through horrific circumstances suffering for the Lord. He did not react like Jeremiah did. He had a balanced view of what had happened to him. Paul goes back and forth with his balanced, God-honoring analysis of the situation. Tell her to note how Paul's right thinking kept him glorifying God instead of blaming God or wallowing in self-pity and despair under very trying circumstances.

> **We are afflicted in every way, but not crushed; perplexed, but not despairing; persecuted, but not forsaken; struck down, but not destroyed; always carrying about in the body the dying of Jesus, so that the life of Jesus also may be manifested in our body. For we who live are constantly being delivered over to death for Jesus' sake, so that the life of Jesus also may be manifested in our mortal flesh. So death works in us, but life in you ... Therefore, we do not lose heart, but though our outer man is decaying, yet our inner man is being renewed day by day. For momentary, light afflicted is producing for us an eternal weight of glory far beyond all comparison, while we look not at the things which are seen, but at the things which are not seen; for the things which are seen are temporal, but the things which are not seen are eternal** (2 Corinthians 4:8-12;16-18).

Biblical Counseling in Practice

Other Counseling Helps

I do not know how many times I have used Jay Adams' "depression spiral" illustration with a counselee, but it has been extremely helpful. The downward spiral represents the point at which something negative happens. It could be a flat tire, or you run out of gas or it could be that something catastrophic happens. Obviously, your emotions will spiral downward. I tell counselees that they likely have done nothing wrong, but the position of the spiral pointing down is a critical point. They can honor God, think, and do the right thing, and thank God for the test. Then their emotions will start on the climb back up. But if they respond sinfully – anger, self-pity, mad at God, or stop doing what they are supposed to be doing – their emotions will spiral down further and further until they end up in the pit of despair. Obviously, it will take a lot longer to move back up to where they should be, but I encourage them that after the Lord teaches them how they should be thinking and responding as they are moving up, they do not ever have to spiral sinfully down again.

Jay Adams' Depression Spiral[24]

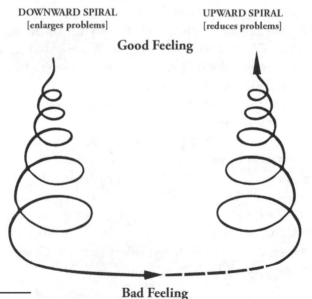

---
[24] Jay Adams. *The Christian Counselor's Manual* (Grand Rapids, Michigan: Zondervan Publishing, 1986).

Counseling Women Who are Depressed

Question your counselee for suicidal thoughts, desires, or plans. The more specific the plan, the more likely she is to carry it out. Even non-specific plans should be taken seriously. Don't ever say to yourself or others, "She is just seeking attention. She won't do it." You do not know that, and it would be better to be safe than sorry.

I have reported several counselees to their families when they had a desire to commit suicide. She would need 24/7 accountability at first. Someone in her family or church family would be ideal. It is a judgment call on your and her family's part, but she may need to be hospitalized in a psychiatric hospital. Most psychiatric hospitals have intake evaluation areas to evaluate the person for admission. If your counselee is that unstable and refuses to go to be evaluated, you can call the police, and they will take her to the emergency room for an evaluation. To commit suicide is against the law, and the emergency room can mandate that she be hospitalized for at least 72 hours against her will.

Here is one word of caution: do not overreact, but pray for wisdom from God. James chapter one promises that He will give it. Most depressed counselees have at some point wished they were dead but tell you, "I don't know how I would do it and I would never do that anyway." If she is telling you the truth, she does not need to be in the hospital but may need for her family to stay with her to help keep her safe.

Specific Instructions for your Counselee[25]

- Fulfill your responsibilities whether you feel like it or not.

- Give her a list of specific responsibilities such as write out a simple menu list, go to the grocery store, cook supper for your family. The meal could be as simple as hot dogs topped with chili from a can and potato chips. But she needs to begin thinking about somebody else besides herself.

---

[25] Free downloads regarding the Gospel – Martha Peace's salvation worksheets on marthapeacetew@blogspot.com and Stuart Scott's Gospel presentation from oneeightycounseling.com.

- If she is alone, have her call you or a relative every morning no later than 8 AM. She is to be out of the bed, showered, and dressed by then. Tell her that if she does not call, you will call the police or her family to check on her.

- Assign her to memorize 1 Thessalonians 5:18 – **"...in everything give thanks; for this is God's will for you in Christ Jesus."**

- Assign her to start a "thankfulness list" and add to it each week.

- For homework, assign her a Self-Talk log. The instructions are to write down what you are thinking when you feel sad, overwhelmed, anxious, or any other painful emotion. When she comes back with her thoughts listed, go over them carefully one-by-one and teach her from the Scriptures how to put off the wrong thoughts and put on true, God-honoring thoughts. For a detailed instruction on how to think biblically, see the *Attitudes of a Transformed Heart* book chapter nine by Martha Peace. One example is renewing your mind from thinking, "I can't take it anymore!" to thinking, "This is a difficult time for me, but God will help me and give me grace to go through it" (1 Corinthians 10:13).

- When she is able, tell her to find someone to start helping, thus taking the focus off herself and on to showing love to others.

- Counsel her to go to her doctor for a complete physical to make sure there is nothing physical contributing to her depression, such as a side effect of her medicine or hypothyroidism.

- Other homework: *Christ and Your Problems* by Jay Adams; *Out of the Blues* by Wayne Mack; A schedule of daily activities. She is to do them regardless of how she feels; Daily Bible Reading in the book of Psalm with instructions to read aloud if she has trouble concentrating; Pray daily and ask God to help her see her sin and responsibility and to help her repent; specific Scripture memory each week.

- Depending on her needs, assign other books to carefully go through with her. Good ones are *Trusting God* by Jerry Bridges and *The Attributes of God* by Arthur Pink.

- A huge contributing factor for your counselee's depression could be anxiety. Because the next chapter in this book is about counseling those with anxiety, I am going to refer you to that chapter.

What happened to Depressed Debbie?

When we began counseling, I met with her twice a week, and her sister came to be with her to hear what I was saying and remind Debbie of those things during the week. Giving Debbie hope was especially helpful for her from the very beginning. Debbie became a Christian soon after the counseling began, and the Scriptures came alive to her. It was, however, difficult at the beginning for her to begin to fulfill her responsibilities, but her mother continued to come over for a few days to be with her and lovingly encourage her to do her work.

Within a fairly short period of time, about six weeks, Debbie was well on her way to becoming stable. She began going to church soon after the counseling began and now is a member of her church and an active participant. After about four weeks of meeting twice a week, we both agreed to change it to once a week. Then after eight weeks, we changed it to every other week for about six sessions.

Does Debbie ever feel depressed and sad now? Of course. Her natural tendency is to feel sorry for herself and to worry. However, when she does that, she now has the biblical understanding and the supernatural grace of God to recover before she spirals down into the pit of despair. Debbie would tell you that instead of her **"tears being her food day and night,"** she is now **"hoping in God and praising Him, her salvation and her God"** (adapted from Psalm 42).

Biblical Counseling in Practice

Chapter Nine

Counseling Women Who Are Anxious

Anxiety is probably the most common problem that I see in counseling. It is also a major contributor to depression. It can be caused by a side effect of medication or a medical problem such as hyperthyroidism. However, it most often results from what a person is thinking. When we worry, it is hard to concentrate on other things. Sometimes it is difficult to eat or difficult to stop eating. Often it is difficult to sleep.

My mother was a worrier and one of the things she worried about was my health; and at various times, she was convinced that I was going to die. As she got older, I was traveling more and speaking at women's conferences. One morning, I had a particularly early flight out of Atlanta and my mother knew that. She could not sleep for worrying about me. So, at 5 AM she called me and said, "I don't want you to go on this trip." I replied, "Good morning, Mother." She proceeded to tell me that she was afraid my plane would crash. So, I replied, "It is rare for planes to crash; but if it does, I will be with the Lord, and He will give you the grace to bear up under it." She replied very nicely, "I knew I couldn't talk to you about this." I smiled to myself and said, "Go back to bed and get some sleep and you will feel better."

What Is Anxiety?

Anxiety is fear that can range from a slight uneasy feeling to a full-blown panic attack. When someone has a panic attack, they become so frightened that the adrenal glands in their body release adrenalin/epinephrine straight into their blood stream. The result is a pounding, rapid heartbeat, rapid breathing, shortness of breath, trembling hands, and a general feeling of terror. This physical reaction is called the "fight or flight response." Proverbs 3:25 calls it **"sudden fear."**

The medical world diagnoses anxiety as a disease or disorder. Certainly, as we have already seen, there can be a physical reaction. There can also be diseases that cause anxiety such as hyperthyroidism or a tumor on the adrenal gland. These diseases are rare, but I do send my counselees to a doctor to have a complete physical. But apart from documentable physical causes, most anxiety is due to a lack of trust in God. People take a concern (real or imagined) and think about it, project it into the future, and jump to a rash/worse possible conclusion. Then they begin to *feel* as if that were happening. Often it becomes a vicious cycle, becoming progressively worse and worse.

People worry about what happened in the past, what is happening now, and what might happen in the future. Researchers have indicated that only about 8% of what people worry about are legitimate concerns. When I counsel a woman with anxiety, I want to hear about her life, struggles, and her walk with the Lord. I teach her basic Bible doctrine such as the Gospel, sanctification, and how to renew her mind with Scripture. For this chapter, I am going to assume I have already been through the basics and am assured as I can be that she is a Christian. I begin with the biblical principles regarding fear.

Biblical Principles Regarding Fear

Our Lord Jesus tells us a story of a wealthy man who went on a journey. Before he left, he gave money to three different servants. Their instructions were to augment the amount of money while he was gone **"…according to his own ability"** (Matthew 25:15). Upon the master's return, the first slave had doubled the original money. The second slave did likewise. The third, who had originally gotten the least amount to begin with, said, **"Master, I knew you to be a hard man, reaping where you did not sow and gathering where you scattered no seed. *And I was afraid*, and went away and hid your talent (money) in the ground. See, you have what is yours"** (Matthew 25:24-25, emphasis mine).

Some might think it was a good excuse for him to be afraid and hide the money. Well, not so. The master's comment to the other two slaves was, **"Well done good and faithful slave. You were faithful with a few things, I will put you in charge of many things; enter into the joy of your master"** (Matthew 25:23). But to the fearful slave the comment was,

> "**You wicked, lazy slave, you knew that I reap where I did not sow and gather where I scattered no seed. Then you ought to have put my money in the bank, and on my arrival I would have received my money back with interest. Therefore take away the talent from him, and give to the one who has the ten talents. For to everyone who has, more shall be given, and he will have an abundance; but from the one who does not have, even what he does have shall be taken away. Throw out the worthless slave into the outer darkness; in that place there will be weeping and gnashing of teeth"** (Matthew 25:26-30).

The point of the parable is to faithfully use the resources God has given us in light of Christ's return. After all that God has done for us, are we are still afraid to use the resources He has given us? So, the first principle regarding fear is: *"Fear keeps us from fulfilling our God-given responsibilities."*

In the Old Testament we learn the story of Abraham whom God chose to bring him out of Ur, a land of idol worshipers, and lead him to a promised land. Abraham followed God not knowing where he would end up. Later it was said of Abraham that he **"believed God and it was reckoned to him as righteousness"** (Genesis 15:6). God gave Abraham great faith and astounding promises, some of which Abraham saw fulfilled in his lifetime. One was the promised son that Sarah, his wife, in her old age would bear. Another was the seemingly impossible test of Abraham's faith when God told him to sacrifice his promised son, Isaac. Abraham believed God and set about to make the sacrifice on Mount Moriah. In a dramatic moment before Abraham could carry out the sacrifice, God called out to him and stopped him. Abraham's faith to obey and trust God at that level was great, and God swore to bless Abraham and his descendants (Genesis chapter 22).

There had been another time before the sacrifice of Isaac test, that Abraham's fear got the best of him. Because of a famine in the land, Abraham and Sarah traveled to Egypt to live temporarily. Abraham became afraid that when Pharaoh saw how exceptionally beautiful Sarah was, he would kill Abraham so he could marry Sarah. So,

Biblical Counseling in Practice

Abraham told Sarah to lie to Pharaoh and say that she was his sister but not mention that she was his wife. Sarah lied, which she should not have done because Abraham asked her to sin. When Pharaoh realized what had happened, he was understandably very angry with Abraham and ordered his men to escort Abraham and Sarah out of Egypt. Abraham's fear overcame his trust in God. The second principle regarding fear is: *"Fear may contribute to a person sinning."*

The Apostle Peter lied and denied knowing our Lord. To me, the story is one of the very saddest in the entire Bible.

> **Now Peter was sitting outside in the courtyard, and a servant-girl came to him and said, "You too were with Jesus the Galilean." But he denied it before them all, saying, "I do not know what you are talking about." When he had gone out to the gateway, another servant-girl saw him and said to those who were there, "This man was with Jesus of Nazareth." And again he denied it with an oath, "I do not know the man." A little later the bystanders came up and said to Peter, "Surely you too are one of them; for even the way you talk gives you away." Then he began to curse and swear, "I do not know the man!" And immediately a rooster crowed, and Peter remembered the word which Jesus had said, "Before a rooster crows, you will deny me three times." And he went out and wept bitterly** (Matthew 26:69-75).

The third principle regarding fear is: *"Fear can cause us to deny our Lord and His Word."*

In one of King David's battles, he was seized by the Philistines, and he wrote a Psalm/poem to remind himself that he could trust God.

> **Be gracious to me, O God, for man has trampled upon me; fighting all day long he oppresses me. My foes have trampled upon me all day long, for they are many who fight proudly against me.** *When I am*

> *afraid, I will put my trust in You. In God, whose word I praise; in God I have put my trust; I shall not be afraid, what can mere man do to me?* (Psalm 56:1-4, emphasis mine).

Often anxious counselees do not have assurance of their salvation. That is because it is difficult for them to trust God and His Word. They may or may not be saved, but if they are not, that is a lack of trust in God also. When David was afraid, he turned his thoughts and petitions to God. He said, **"I will put my trust in You."** So, the fourth principle regarding fear is: *"The biblical antidote to fear is* trusting *God."*

After you teach the biblical principles of fear, teach them very practical solutions to implement in their hearts (thinking) and outwardly to others.

Practical Bible Solutions to Fear

The Apostle Peter was opposed by the Apostle Paul for his deception. When the Jewish believers came to Galatia, Peter stopped eating meals with the Gentile Christians. What he did was not just a preference of who to eat with, but the Gospel itself was at stake. When Paul wrote to the church at Galatia, he explained the problem.

> **But when Cephas [Peter] came to Antioch, I opposed him to his face, because he stood condemned. For prior to the coming of certain men from James; he used to eat with the Gentiles; but when they came, he began to withdraw and hold himself aloof, fearing the party of the circumcision… But when I (Paul) saw that they were not straightforward about the truth of the Gospel, I said to Cephas in the presence of all, "If you being a Jew live like the Gentiles and not like the Jews, how is it that you compel the Gentiles to live like Jews? We are Jews by nature and not sinners from among the Gentiles; nevertheless knowing that a man is not justified by**

the works of the Law [the unsaved Jews believed that Gentiles were unclean and therefore would not eat with them] **but through faith in Christ Jesus...** (Galatians 2:11-12, 14-16, explanation mine).

Peter was a complete hypocrite and he got caught. Anyone who is deceptive, or a liar must always be afraid of getting caught. *Sin will cause you to be a hypocrite.*

Jacob and his mother deceived his brother Esau and his father Isaac, thus, stealing Esau's birthright from him. Esau threatened to kill Jacob but only after their father, Isaac, died. Later, Isaac did die, and Jacob ran away and fled to his Uncle Laban's home. Years later, God told Jacob to go home. By that time, Jacob had two wives and their maids, many children plus herds of animals. He never forgot his brother's threat to kill him. On the journey home he wrestled with the Angel of the Lord and his hip was injured, so he limped and could no longer walk or run. Also, he had women, children, and animals with him. If that was not difficult enough, a messenger came to him to report that Esau was on his way to meet him with an army of 400 men! He was very afraid for good reason, so he prayed and reminded himself of God's promises:

> **Jacob said, "O God of my father Abraham and God of my father Isaac O LORD, who said to me, 'Return to your country and to your relatives and I will prosper you,' ... Deliver me, I pray, from the hand of my brother, from the hand of Esau; for I fear him, that he will come and attack me and the mothers with the children. For You said, 'I will surely prosper you and make your descendants as the sand of the sea, which is too great to be numbered' ..."** (Genesis 32:7,9).

A lesson we can learn from this story is instead of panicking in fear, *remind yourself of God's promises and keep obeying Him.*

Part of counseling is to *teach your counselee to be wise and make responsible decisions* such as sticking to her budget. If she overspends, she will have to worry about how to pay her bills. If she is wise, she

"**...will walk securely and** [her] **foot will not stumble, when** [she] **lies down,** [her] **sleep will be sweet**" (Proverbs 23-24, adaptation mine).

In Paul's second letter to his spiritual son, Timothy, he exhorts him to not be afraid but to "**... kindle afresh the gift of God which is in you through the laying on of my hands. For God has not given us a spirit of timidity, but of power and love and discipline**" (2 Timothy 1:6-7). *So, explain to your counselee that she, too, has the power of God working in her to give her grace to face her fears.*

Fear is very self-focused but to counter our self-focus, Jesus said we are to love God (by obeying His commands) and love others (by being patient, kind, etc.) (Matthew 22:35-40; 1 Corinthians 13:4-7). Explain to your counselee that she must deliberately turn her thoughts and focus from herself to God and others. It will not be easy for her because she will not *feel* like it, but the more she goes against how she feels and changes her thoughts to God-honoring right thoughts and does the right thing, eventually she will feel better. God promises His peace. *So, she is to do what is right whether she feels like it or not. Thus, she will show love to God by obeying Him.*

In the beginning, one very practical assignment you can give to your counselee is Scripture memory. It does not have to be long passages, but I would have her memorize easy passages such as:

> **Praise the LORD! How blessed is the man who fears the LORD, who greatly delights in His commands** (Psalm 112:1).
>
> **When I am afraid, I will put my trust in You** (Psalm 56:3).
>
> **Even though I walk through the valley of the shadow of death, I fear no evil, for You are with me; Your rod and Your staff, they comfort me** (Psalm 23:4).
>
> **Do not be wise in your own eyes; fear the LORD and turn away from evil** (Proverbs 3:7).

> **I sought the LORD, and He answered me, and delivered me from all my fears** (Psalm 34:4).
>
> **No temptation has overtaken you but such as is common to man; and God is faithful, who will not allow you to be tempted beyond what you are able, but with the temptation will provide the way of escape also, so that you will be able to endure it** (1 Corinthians 10:13).
>
> **Therefore, let us draw near with confidence to the throne of grace, so that we may receive mercy and find grace to help in time of need** (Hebrews 4:16).

The following is a longer passage but very practical as we will see in the next section of this chapter.

> **Be anxious for nothing, but in everything by prayer and supplication, with thanksgiving let your requests be made known to God. And the peace of God, which surpasses all comprehension, will guard your hearts and your minds in Christ Jesus. Finally, brethren, whatever is true, whatever is honorable, whatever is right, whatever is pure, whatever is lovely, whatever is of good repute, if there is any excellence and if anything worthy of praise, dwell on these things. The things you have learned and received and heard and seen in me, practice these things, and the God of peace will be with you** (Philippians 4:6-9).

Biblical Prayer, Thoughts, and Actions

A helpful exercise to help your counselee identify her fear is to have her do a self-talk log. Instruct her to write down what she is thinking every time she feels anxious. You probably will not have to ask her to do a self-talk log more than a couple of times, as most people tend to think the same anxious thoughts over and over. When she comes back with her thoughts written down or listed on her cell phone, note them in your records. What she is thinking is what is going on in her heart. Telling her to stop thinking those thoughts is not going to be enough. You must show her how with lots of examples.

Anxiety Journal

Explain that the anxiety journal is based on Philippians 4:6-9. Each entry is comprised of one thought, three entry parts (a prayer, a mind-renewed thought, and biblical actions), and will take up about one page in her notebook. Place the original thought at the top of the page, and here is an example:

[Original thought] "I just know that something horrible is going to happen."

1. **Biblical Prayer** has two aspects based on Philippians 4:6-7. The two parts of the prayer are a supplication, which is a humble request, and expressed thanksgiving to God.
    Father,
    My request is [based on her original thought] that nothing horrible will happen in my life *if* that would glorify You the most.
    Thank You for reminding me how much I need You.
    In Jesus Name, Amen

2. **Biblical Thought** based on Philippians 4:8. Paul lists the kinds of thoughts we are to let dwell in our mind. Examples are:

    True, thoughts you know to be a fact, not exaggerated or underplayed; **Honorable,** God-honoring thoughts; **Excellent and Praiseworthy,** thoughts that point to God

    (For a more detailed explanation of the list in Philippians 4:8, see chapter nine in *Attitudes of a Transformed Heart*.)[26]

---
[26] Peace, Martha. *Attitudes of a Transformed Heart* (Bemidji, MN: Focus Publishing, 2002), p.125-144.

Suggest that to make thoughts true and God-honoring, a substitute thought could be:
Nothing horrible is happening (true), but if in the unlikely event it did, God would *at that time* give me grace to bear up under it (God honoring) (1 Corinthians 10:13).

3. **Biblical Actions** based on Philippians 4:9. The actions are a list of practical things to do, such as daily Bible reading in Psalms, working on Scripture memory such as Psalm 34:4, **"I sought the LORD, and He answered me, and delivered me from all my fears."** An important biblical action is daily prayer and adding more anxious thoughts to add to her anxiety journal will be helpful. Another action would be to read Arthur Pink's book, *The Attributes of God*. Instruct her to read one chapter every week and look up in her own Bible the Scriptures that Pink quotes or sites. She should have a dictionary handy to look up any words he uses that she does not know. He uses big words!

Point out to her the astounding hope in the Philippians 4:6-9 passage. **"The peace of God...will guard her heart and her mind"** (Philippians 4:7). Also, **"the God of peace will be with you"** (Philippians 4:9). What wonderful, practical, and amazing promises especially for someone who is afraid!

Conclusion

After a few weeks of meeting with you, your counselee should more often be thinking true and God-honoring thoughts and not be nearly so panicked. Her anxiety has come from her heart and is basically a lack of trust in God. God, in His kindness, gave us clear instructions in the Scriptures to help us to trust Him as she **"... humbles [her]self under the mighty hand of God, that He may exalt [her] at the proper time, casting all [her] anxiety on Him, because He cares for [her]"** (1 Peter 5:6-7 adaptation mine).

There *are* biblical, very practical antidotes to the painful emotions. Your counselee *can* show love to God (by obeying His Word) and love to others (by fulfilling her responsibilities). God will help her overcome her painful emotions as her mind is renewed to think true, right, God-honoring thoughts and to fulfill her responsibilities whether she feels like it or not.

Biblical Counseling in Practice

Chapter Ten

Counseling Women to be Godly Mothers

One day when our daughter Anna was about three years old, she came to me and said, "Mama, I'll never get married." I was surprised and asked, "Why, Honey?" "Because," she answered, "I will never leave you." I replied, "Oh Anna, you might change your mind someday." Well, of course she did! When I think about this story, it reminds me how precious and how truly short the time is with our children.

If our children are doing well spiritually and otherwise, there are many wonderful joys in being a parent. The Apostle John wrote about his joy upon hearing about his spiritual children doing well: **"I have no greater joy than this, to hear of my children walking in the truth"** (3 John:4). If they are not doing well, the grief and sorrow may be extreme as **"a foolish son is a grief to his Mother"** (Proverbs 10:1; 17:25).

It is common for mothers to seek biblical counsel and advice, to feel overwhelmed with the burden of childcare, to worry about their children, to be devastated because of something the child has done or because their child is not saved. Whatever the concerns are, we must remember that there are two sinners in a mother-child relationship, and they are interacting very closely. One may be a two-year-old and the other acting like a two-year-old. They need hope, realistic biblical goals, and practical God-honoring solutions to their problems.

In this chapter, I want to cover three areas: the goal for the Christian parent, a right understanding of the Gospel and salvation of the child, and six common problems for which mothers seek biblical counsel with practical tips on how to counsel them.

The Goal for the Christian Parent

The goal for the Christian parent is to be faithful to God's Word by His grace and for His glory. Faithfulness, not perfection, is rewarded by the Lord. A faithful parent strives to honor the Lord in parenting, repenting, and changing. They trust God and His Word. They glorify God by fulfilling their biblical responsibility to bring their children up in the (1) discipline of the Lord and (2) the instruction of the Lord (Ephesians 6:4).

A Right Understanding of the Gospel and the Child's Salvation[27]

Children should be taught the Gospel in its context. There is not one Gospel for adults and another for children. If God is opening the child's eyes to the truth, they will truly comprehend the basics of the Gospel. Stuart Scott calls this, "adult-like content with child-like faith."

> **And there is salvation in no one else; for there is no other name under heaven that has been given among men by which we must be saved** (Acts 4:12).
>
> **Now I make known to you, brethren, the Gospel which I preached to you, which also you received, in which also you stand, by which also you are saved, if you hold fast the word which I preached to you, unless you believed in vain. For I delivered to you as of first importance what I also received, that Christ died for our sins according to the Scripture, and that He was buried, and that He was raised on the third day according to the Scriptures, and that He appeared to Cephas, then to the twelve... For as in Adam all die, so also in Christ all will be made alive** (1 Corinthians 15:1-5,22).
>
> **Moreover, I will give you a new heart and put a new spirit within you; and I will remove the heart of stone from your flesh and give you a heart of flesh. I will put My Spirit within you and cause you to walk in my statues, and you will be careful to observe my ordinances** (Ezekiel 36:26-27).

---

[27] Peace, Martha and Scott, Stuart. *The Faithful Parent* (Phippsburg, NJ: P&R Publishing, 2010).

Children should be taught a biblical understanding of God. He is our Creator and highest authority. He is the authority over the child *and* his parents.

> **Know that the LORD Himself is God; it is He who has made us, and not we ourselves; We are His people and the sheep of His pasture** (Psalm 100:3).
>
> **In the beginning God created the heavens and the earth** (Genesis 1:1).

Tell them about the Trinity, one God in three Persons – God the Father, God the Son, and God the Holy Spirit.

> **After being baptized, Jesus came up immediately from the water; and behold, the heavens were opened, and he saw the Spirit of God descending as a dove and lighting on Him, and behold, a voice out of the heavens said, "This is My beloved Son, in whom I am well-pleased"** (Matthew 3:16-17).

Explain to the child that God is unique. There is no one like Him. He has always existed.

> **To you it was shown that you might know that the LORD, He is God; there is no other besides Him** (Deuteronomy 4:35).

Teach the child that God is holy, and He wants us to be holy. That means to obey Him perfectly and not sin.

> **As obedient children, do not be conformed to the former lusts which were yours in your ignorance, but like the Holy One who called you, be holy yourselves also in all your behavior; because it is written, "You shall be holy, for I am holy"** (1 Peter 14-16).

Children should understand that they sin, and our sin is worse than we think it is. Sin is when we think and do things that God says is wrong, and we are not to do them. Theologians call this total depravity. It does not mean that every person will be as bad as possible, but that every part of every person (mind, will, and emotions) is affected by sin.

> **Therefore, just as through one man sin entered into the world, and death through sin, and so death spread to all men, because all sinned ...** (Romans 5:12).

> **All of us like sheep have gone astray, each of us has turned to his own way...** (Isaiah 53:6).

Explain to the children that there is nothing *they* can do to take themselves out from under God's wrath. Only God can do that by His grace, love, and mercy. Therefore, be careful not to imply that young children are already in a personal relationship with God before they have responded to the Gospel. Also, be careful not to unsettle young children with the harsh realities of their unsaved state (eternal hell) before they can grasp the Gospel truth.

> **For Christ also died for sins once for all, the just for the unjust, so that He might bring us to God, having been put to death in the flesh, but made alive in the spirit** (1 Peter 3:18).

> **But when the kindness of God our Savior and His love for mankind appeared, He saved us, not on the basis of deeds which we have done in righteousness, but according to His mercy, by the washing of regeneration and renewing by the Holy Spirit, whom He poured out upon us richly through Jesus Christ our Savior, so that being justified by His grace we would be made heirs according to the hope of eternal life** (Titus 3:4-7).

The evidence of salvation is not just a prayer prayed, but a new heart that turns *from* sin *to* Christ and continues to persevere by God's grace. They now live for **"Him who died and rose again on their behalf"** (2 Corinthians 5:15).

But what about …?

- But what about pressuring a child to make a commitment? Instead, trust God that He will save His chosen in His time.

  But as many as received Him, to them He gave the right to become children of God, even to those who believe in His name, who were born, not of blood nor of the will of the flesh nor of the will of man, but of God (John 1:12-13).

- But what about a child who makes a profession of faith but does not live like a Christian until later in life, then rededicates their life? The Scriptures do not teach anything like this.

  Therefore if anyone is in Christ, he is a new creature; the old things passed away; behold, new things have come (2 Corinthians 5:17).

- But what about the promise of Proverbs 22:6, **"Train up a child in the way he should go, even when he is old he will not depart from it."** Some people think this is an ironclad promise, but Proverbs are general truths not ironclad promises. In general, a child brought up in the discipline and instruction of the Lord will live a Christian life and not depart from it.

- But what about disciplining children who are saved? Certainly, teach them Bible doctrine such as how the Gospel applies to their daily lives, and what it means to be "in (union) with Christ" and how that is lived out. Also, teach them what and how to pray and worship and share their faith, how to renew their minds, decision making from a biblical perspective, and how by God's grace to put off sin and put on righteousness. Parents are to raise all their children, saved or unsaved, in the **"…discipline and instruction of the Lord"** (Ephesians 6:4).

Those are the main questions that mothers have asked me. So, now we turn to six typical problems that mothers face and their practical, biblical counseling solutions.

Problems and Solutions

Impatient Mother

One of the main challenges for a mother is being patient with her children. There could be a long-standing habit/pattern of sinful anger. Ask the question, "When you are impatient, what happens?" Her answer may be that she snaps at them verbally, grabs them in anger or is sarcastic. Ask, "Is it worse when it is time for your period?" Sin issues are usually exaggerated when it is time for her period. Another question to ask is, "Typically, what would your child be doing when you become impatient?"

Assign her to write a self-talk log. Instruct her that this is not a journal about how she feels. It is a list of thoughts that she is thinking when she feels irritated or frustrated with her child. Teach her that impatience is a lack of love, as love *is* patient. It is also pride in the mother's heart by not accepting God's sovereign plan over her life.

Ask her to go over each of her thoughts and point out her responsibilities before God. These are to ask God's forgiveness, pray and ask Him to make her into a gentle, loving mother, to help her think in a loving way, and to respond in love. In Titus 2:4-7 the older more mature women are to teach and admonish the younger women to **"love their children."** That kind of love is *philos* love, meaning to think of the child as a dear, beloved person that you cherish.

Instruct her to put on loving thoughts and to put off her impatient thoughts.

Examples:

Impatient Thoughts	Loving Thoughts (based on 1 Corinthians 13:4-7)
1. "That really irritates me."	"How does God want me to respond?" **Love does not take into account a wrong suffered.**

Counseling Women to be Godly Mothers

2. "That makes me angry."	**Love is not provoked.** "I can show love to her in spite of her sin."
3. (In a harsh tone) "You're too slow, I'll tie your shoe for you."	**Love is patient.** "I can show love to him by waiting a few seconds while he tries to tie his shoe."
4. "I've got more important things to do than listen to her whine."	"Her whining is a sinful form of communication. My responsibility is to train her to speak in a sweet tone of voice." **Love rejoices in righteousness.**
5. "I wish he would leave me alone!"	"He's only two years old. I'm going to let him help me even if it takes twice as long." **Love is kind.**

Exhort her to be discerning about her sinful thoughts, confess those thoughts as they occur as sin, ask God to forgive her, and replace the sinful thought with a God-honoring and loving others response. God will, in turn, give her grace (power) to obey Him and to change. It will probably seem mechanical at first especially because it is not her "natural" way to think, but eventually God will change her character if she persists.

> **But have nothing to do with worldly fables fit only for old women. On the other hand, discipline yourself** [do or think the right thing over and over] **for the purpose of godliness; for bodily discipline is only of little profit, but godliness is profitable for all things, since it holds promise for the present life and also for the life to come** (1 Timothy 4:7, explanation mine).

> **All Scripture is inspired by God and profitable for teaching** [tell us what to do right], **for reproof** [tell us what we are doing wrong], **for correction** [biblically how to correct it], **for training in righteousness** [doing it over and over until you get it right the first time];

so that the man of God may be adequate, equipped for every good work (2 Timothy 3:16-17, explanation mine).

... in reference to your former manner of life, you lay aside the old self, which is being corrupted in accordance with the lusts of deceit, and that you be renewed in the spirit of your mind, and put on the new self, which in the likeness of God has been created in righteousness and holiness of the truth (Ephesians 4:22-24).

When a counselee is impatient with her children, there are additional issues to explore. Does the mother allow herself enough time to get ready and avoid putting unnecessary pressure on herself? Is she unorganized so that she does not know where her car keys are or her child's shoes? If she is not organized, she is setting herself up for failure. For example, does she get up early enough in the morning to not have to rush? If a mom does not get up earlier than her children and get dressed, she does not stand much of a chance of avoiding frustration with her day and with them.

Does the mother understand that there may be times she is providentially hindered by God when her child falls and scrapes his knee or spills his milk? She will have to stop what she is doing and help her child. She will also have to stop what she is doing to discipline and correct her child. Help her to consider that frustrating situations are God's way of testing her to see *her* obedience to Him.

Does she appropriately discipline the first time her child either disobeys or obeys with a bad attitude such as whining? Your counselee should speak to and correct her child while she herself is speaking in a normal tone of voice. She should make sure she has the child's attention, and her instructions are age-appropriate for the child. If she ends up telling him repeatedly, she will likely end up irritated and raising her voice. That is her fault, not the child's fault. She needs to correct and discipline him the *first* time he disobeys. (For further tips on discipline and spanking, see *The Faithful Parent* by Martha Peace and Stuart Scott.)[28]

[28] Ibid, Chapter Two.

Cruel and Malicious to Her Children

Your counselee may only casually mention that she becomes angry. Don't downplay it and say, "I'm sure you are a good mother. All mothers become frustrated from time to time." She may be downplaying how bad it really is. Find out what she means when she says, "I'm not a very good mother" or "Sometimes I get angry at my kids." She may be using anger and cruelty to control the child or to take out her frustrations on her children. She may punish them in wicked ways. Her speech may be abusive. As a counselor, you need to have a clear picture of what is really happening. Ask her, "Give me some examples of when you are not a good mother." Do not assume anything.

Teach her Bible doctrine regarding malice and abusive speech. When I think of malice, I think of meanness and cruelty, perhaps wishing ill will. Abusive speech is "obscene or derogatory speech intended to hurt and wound someone."[29] The Scriptures are clear that we are to put off anger, wrath, malice, slander, and abusive speech. We are to put on **"a heart of compassion, kindness, humility, gentleness and patience; bearing with one another, and forgiving each other…"** (Colossians 3:8, 12-13).

Explain that her motive must be to glorify God and to discipline and instruct her child in a righteous manner (1 Corinthians 10:31). Tell her, "You do not say cruel, means things to your child because it is sinful, evil, and offensive to God. It is a deed of the flesh (Galatians 5:20). It also could easily provoke a child to anger (Ephesians 6:4). If you have sinned against your child this way, ask God's forgiveness, the child's forgiveness, and figure out what you should have said instead."

Remind your counselee that she was saved according to the mercy of God and that malice and being hateful should no longer characterize her life. She should be full of mercy and easy to be entreated. Even if her child is sinning wickedly, she does not have to. She can overcome evil with good, not by being more evil. She can be merciful like God Himself who is **"kind to the ungrateful and evil"** (Luke 6:35-36). We are to be merciful as He is merciful. (See also Titus 3:2-7, James 3:17, Romans 12:21, and Luke 6:35-36).

---

[29] MacArthur, John, *Commentary on Colossians*, p.144.

Biblical Counseling in Practice

She must by God's grace put off malice and abusive speech and instead be kind and tender-hearted.

Let all bitterness and wrath and anger and clamor and slander be put away from you, along with all malice. Be kind to one another, tender-hearted, forgiving each other, just as God in Christ also has forgiven you (Ephesians 4:31-32).

Malicious and Abusive Speech	Kind, Tender-Hearted, and Forgiving Speech
1. "You're stupid."	"I know this is difficult, but I want you to patiently try again. It is more important that you show love (love is patient) by trying than it is that you can do it correctly."
2. "You are such a slob; you make me sick!"	"Your room is not cleaned as well as it should be. Perhaps I have not taught you as well as I should have. Let me show you again."
3. "I wish you had never been born!"	"You are a blessing to us from God. I love you but I am going to discipline you because you did not obey."

A mother like this will probably need close accountability. Perhaps a combination of her husband when he is home, and one of the older ladies in the church when he is not. If she is so cruel verbally, she may also be physically cruel far beyond a normal spanking. As her counselor, you have an obligation to protect her children. If the children are in danger physically, you may need to involve Family and Children's Services and/or the police. It is very grievous to contact the authorities, but you have a moral obligation to protect the children. It is assault and battery to beat the children. If she is married, the husband should be made aware of her actions. It would be wise to consult a lawyer if you are unsure of what to do. Regardless, you will need to come forward as a witness to the appropriate authorities. (See Romans 13:1-2.)

Child-Centered Home

A mother who oversees a child-centered home seems overly concerned about pleasing her child. She does not discipline her child as she should when the child is disrespectful, and she gives into him even when she believes it is not wise. The child manipulates the mother by whining, anger, crying, begging, pouting in a power play over clothes, food, bedtime, etc. A spoiled child like this is not grateful to his parents and likely angry if he does not have his way. He may say ugly remarks like, "I hate you." In addition, the child may be permitted to make decisions that are inappropriate for that age child to make.

Explain to the mother a biblical view of love. Love gives the child what he *needs,* not necessarily what he *wants*. Especially for the younger children, disobedience and disrespect are the occasion for a spanking. **"He who withholds his rod hates his son, but he who loves him disciplines him diligently"** (Proverbs 13:24). This *is* showing love like God does as He disciplines those whom He loves (Hebrews 12:6).

Some mothers think giving in to their child (when they really should not) is showing mercy. They tell me, "I have the gift of mercy. And I feel so badly for him (when he is suffering the consequences of his behavior)." Some will bail their child out when he should be facing the consequences of his sin. The mother thinks, "I just want him to be happy." Or "I know I should not give in, but I can't help it. I have the gift of mercy." Explain to her that Godly discipline *is* merciful. The true gift of mercy does not use the "gift" as an excuse to justify sin, and as a rule, remove consequences from the child.

Counsel the mother on the biblical view of how to help a child become a mature person. She may have been wrongly influenced by our culture and the psychological models. She may say things like, "I want him to feel good about himself no matter what he has done." Or she may use positive reinforcement in an unbiblical, manipulative way or be concerned about his significance and security needs. If she is, then teach her the biblically correct way to think. The child's purpose on earth is to glorify God and to serve his family as he is able, at whatever level of maturity in life. If in the process, he is sinned against, then he is to forgive and overcome evil with good. Our Lord Jesus said, **"For if you forgive others for their transgressions, your heavenly**

Father will also forgive you" (Matthew 6:14). And the Apostle Paul wrote, **"we are to overcome evil with good"** (Romans 12:21). A mother does not have to artificially manipulate her child so that he will *feel* a certain way. She needs to point him to the Lord. That is his purpose in life.

Idolatrous Emotional Attachments (The world calls this co-dependency.)

I am defining idolatrous emotional attachments as a mother using her child in an unbiblical manner to try to feel better about her hurts and problems. Point her to God and to her responsibility to be a mature mother instead of being selfishly, emotionally dependent on her children in a way that God never intended.

> **Trust in the LORD with all your heart and do not lean on your own understanding** (Proverbs 3:5).
>
> **Therefore if you have been raised up with Christ, keep seeking the things above, where Christ is, seated at the right hand of God. Set your mind on the things above, not on the things that are on earth** (Colossians 3:1-2).

Exhort her to be like the Psalmist in Psalm 94:19. **"When my anxious thoughts multiply within me, your consolations delight my soul."** Help her realize that no man, not even her child, can provide the refuge and relief she is seeking. Scripture has a warning for her in Psalm 118:8: **"It is better to take refuge in the LORD than to trust in princes."**

Below are some examples of counseling situations and tips on how to respond.

Examples of Idolatrous Emotional Attachments	Counseling Tips
Mother may share hurts and problems with the child as if they were an adult. Uses child like a husband or best girlfriend by pouring her heart out about her husband or someone who has hurt her. Example – husband may be an alcoholic or an adulterer or irresponsible with money. The results are the child feels an incredible burden of responsibility to make everything all right for Mom but has no power to do so. The child may take up an offense for the mother and become very bitter towards the person who has hurt her. Or the child may have magical thinking such as "If I am a good girl, my daddy won't do these things."	The correct way for the mother to respond: if the child is old enough to be aware of what is happening, the mother should factually give a limited amount of information and at the same time give the child hope. They can pray for the father together, but she should not use the child as a "sounding board" to vent her feelings nor give the child unnecessary data. Also, be sure to follow up with any positive encouragement.
Mother may use guilt to manipulate the child to have her way (an unbiblical way to control her child). Example: "I knew you couldn't do anything right." "Go ahead (but is looking mournful and sighing while speaking)." "I thought you loved me." "I give up (sighing)." "You don't care about me." "I couldn't bear it if you didn't do what I wanted."	Instead of using guilt, the mother should be straightforward in her requests or instructions to the child: "You may go." "You may not go." Or "I will think about it and let you know on Wednesday."

Mother may worry or be fearful that the child may die or be injured. Thinks about it and jumps to a rash conclusion and tells herself thoughts like "I couldn't bear it if anything happened." Mother is overly protective and shares her concern with her child.	Teach her that she must trust God that if something did happen God would give her the grace to go through it (1Corinthians 10:13).
Feels deeply hurt if child sins or disobeys her. Judges the child's motives. "You did that deliberately to hurt me."	Teach her that children are born with "folly in their hearts" and they are born in sin and they do sin. Her responsibility is to not be surprised when they do sin and to biblically discipline and instruct the child, and not play it over and over in her mind what the child did and thus become bitter towards her child. Remind her that she may not always see immediate fruit, but *she* is to be faithful (1 Corinthians 13:4-7; Ephesians 6:1-4).

As you counsel a struggling mother, you may discover that she ...

Lacks Appropriate Reproof and Instruction Skills

Teach the mother to train her children to respond respectfully. That includes her children's tone of voice, their countenance, and the words they say. This training begins when they are old enough to talk and continues as they get older. A four-year-old pitching a fit when he does not get his way becomes the sixteen-year-old cursing her when he does not get his way. It is the same fool's heart. A fool will not listen; he only wants to have his way.

Children learn early in life how to manipulate their parents to get their way. If they cannot have their way, they can at least punish the parent in the process. Whatever the child's age, the mother should remain calm, speak in a normal tone of voice, and give the child clear instructions such as, "I will not let you speak to me that way. What should you have said?" If the child says the right words but has a "look that would kill" on his face, then the mother should say, "The words are good. Now say them again with a pleasant look on your face." If he does not cooperate with the training, then if he is a younger child, spank him. If he is older, send him to what Lou Priolo [Director of Competent to Counsel International and Director of Biblical Counseling at Christ Covenant Buckhead in Atlanta] calls the "think room." That is a room where he has nothing to do except think about how he *should* have responded. Once he figures that out, he can come back and start the conversation over. That way, the mother is fulfilling her responsibility to discipline and instruct him in the Lord.

If the child is an unbeliever, teach the mother to give an age-appropriate Gospel to the child. Not a vague, fuzzy meaningless Gospel such as "If you want to go to Heaven, ask Jesus into your heart." But tell them the truth, "God is holy, and you are not …" If the child is older and professes Christ, confront the child privately with his sin. If he does not repent, then she should bring in other witnesses. Depending on the seriousness of the child's sin, the steps of church discipline may need to be followed. (See Matthew 18:15-18.)

Another reproof skill the mother should teach her children is how to reprove *her* but do it in a respectful way. When that happens, the mother should humbly admit her sin, if in fact she has sinned, and ask God's forgiveness and the child's forgiveness. This is so important because children are forgiving, but it really provokes them to anger when a parent is arrogant and will not admit their faults.

One last issue that I have seen with counseling mothers is an …

Unbiblical Atmosphere in the Home

Help the mother to see her responsibility to **"smile at the future"** (Proverbs 31:25). Instead of being depressed and anxious about the future, she should be grateful to God and look forward to what God is going to do in her life and her child's life. Even if she is in a difficult situation, she has hope and that will give the child hope.

In addition to giving the mother hope, hold her accountable to sing, laugh, hug, and kiss her children. Ask her, "how are you doing?" There should be a lot of joy and fun in the home. The mother should be expressive and freely express her gratitude to the Lord for their blessings and His goodness even in the face of adversity. Her children should see the joy on her face when she talks about the Lord.

Teach her that the atmosphere in her home should reflect that the everyday ordinary Christian life is one of great joy and not oppression, nor a burden to obey a list of rules and regulations. 1 John 5:3 tells us, **"For this is the love of God, that we keep His commandments. And His commandments are not burdensome."**

Conclusion

Biblical counselors can help a mother in God-honoring, practical ways. Mothers need hope and their goal should be **"to be faithful to God's Word by His grace and for His glory."** No matter the age of the child, the mother can have hope that *she* can be faithful regardless of the child's salvation status or his struggles. As she strives to bring her child up in the **"discipline and instruction of the Lord"** (Ephesians 6:1-4), she is honoring her Lord and giving Him great glory.

Chapter Eleven

Counseling Women Going Through a Divorce

In my years of counseling women, it was difficult to work with women who were going through a divorce because their emotional pain was always so great. Often, they felt overwhelmed. The wife may not know what is really happening. She is sometimes confused, hurt, guilt-laden, scared, angry, grieving, self-pitying, and desperate, even if she is a Christian. Very often there are huge financial problems and not enough money to pay the bills, much less hire a lawyer. The children are upset, and her parents are grieved and/or angry. At various times, everyone involved wants revenge. Divorce is often worse than a death. It is embarrassing, humiliating, devastating, and it *always* breaks a vow made before God on the part of one or both.

For this chapter, we are going to presume three elements to be true. The first is that there are only two biblical grounds for divorce—adultery and the unbeliever departing (Matthew 19:9; 1 Corinthians 7:15). If you have questions about biblical grounds for divorce, I highly recommend Jim Newheiser's book, *Marriage, Divorce, and Remarriage: Critical Questions and Answers*.[30]

The second presumption is that if a wife is divorcing her husband, and she does not have clear biblical grounds and will not repent, she should be disciplined by her church (Matthew 18:15-18). Finally, for this chapter, we will presume the wife is a Christian and thus wants to do what is right, give glory to God, and wisely fight for her marriage.

In researching this chapter, I did a brief survey of the help offered by Christian Psychology. Basically, what I found is an emphasis on the wife's wounds, inner pains, needs, and feelings of worthlessness. It was all very man-centered and encouraged the wife to have a self-focus. But instead, we will take the God-centered, instead of man-centered, approach. Remind your counselee of the big-picture: "God is our Creator. We are His creatures here to serve Him and give Him glory" (1 Corinthians 10:31).

---

[30] Newheiser, Jim. *Marriage, Divorce, and Remarriage: Critical Questions and Answers* (Phippsburg, NY: P&R Publishing, 2017).

Encourage the wife to think, "My responsibility is to love God perfectly by obeying His Word with a heart's desire to please Him and to love others by being patient, kind, not provoked to anger, etc." (Matthew 22:36-39). Help her understand that all we think or do, including a divorce, should be a reflection back on the goodness of God. He makes such a trial bearable and purposeful instead of empty and vain.

She should not think in terms of "forgiving God" for her situation. That is blasphemy as we have nothing to forgive God for. It reminds me of Romans 9:20, **"Who are you, O man, who answers back to God?"** Do we dare shake our fist at God after all He has done and is doing for us? Instead, she could think, "This is hard, and I am scared to find out what is really going on, but God will help me each step of the way and only give me what I can bear (by His grace) at the moment" (1 Corinthians 10:13; 1 Peter 5:6,7).

As her counselor, pray *for* her and she can pray *for herself* that:
- She will give God glory.

> **Whether then, you eat or drink or whatever you do, do all to the glory of God.** (1 Corinthians 10:31).

- God will comfort her.

> **Blessed be the God and Father of our Lord Jesus Christ, the Father of mercies and God of all comfort, who comforts us in all our afflictions so that we will be able to comfort those who are in any affliction with the comfort with which we ourselves are comforted by God** (2 Corinthians 1:3-4).

- Her affections will be set on the things above.

> **Therefore, if you have been raised up with Christ, keep seeking the things above, where Christ is, seated at the right hand of God. Set your mind on things above, not on the things that are on earth** (Colossians 3:1-2).

Counseling Women Going Through a Divorce

- God will protect her and the children.

  But the Lord is faithful, and He will strengthen and protect you from the evil one (2 Thessalonians 3:3).

- God will provide financially for her and the children.

  Pray, then, in this way: ... Give us this day our daily bread (Matthew 6:9,11).

- She will bear fruit for the Lord through the process.

  But the fruit of the Spirit is love, joy, peace, patience, kindness, goodness, faithfulness, gentleness, self-control ... (Galatians 5:22).

- She will think and respond by facing reality and not being naive or foolish.

  Finally, brethren, whatever is true ... (Philippians 4:8).

- She will not go through this in vain and end up angry, bitter, and self-focused on "my needs, my worth, my esteem."

  Therefore, since Christ has suffered in the flesh, arm yourselves also with the same purpose, because he who has suffered in the flesh has ceased from sin, so as to live the rest of the time in the flesh no longer for the lusts of men, but for the will of God (1 Peter: 4:1-2).

- She will be anxious for nothing.

  Be anxious for nothing, but in everything by prayer and supplication with thanksgiving let your requests be made known to God. And the peace of God, which surpasses all comprehension, will guard your hearts and your minds in Christ Jesus (Philippians 4:6-7).

- She will be wise.

  My son if you will receive my words, and treasure my commandments within you, make your ear attentive to wisdom, incline your heart to understanding; for if you cry for discernment, lift your voice for understanding; if you seek her as silver and search for her as for hidden treasures; then you will discern the fear of the Lord and discover the knowledge of God. For the LORD gives wisdom; from His mouth come knowledge and understanding. He stores up sound wisdom for the upright; He is a shield to those who walk in integrity... (Proverbs 2:1-7).

- She will think rightly and **"hate evil, love good ..."** (Amos 5:15).

- She will be content.

  But godliness actually is a means of great gain when accompanied by contentment. For we have brought nothing into the world, so we cannot take anything out of it either. If we have food and covering, with these we shall be content (1 Timothy 6:6-8).

- She will keep a good conscience.

  Who is there to harm you if you prove zealous for what is good? But even if you should suffer for the sake of righteousness, you are blessed. And do not fear their intimidation, and do not be troubled, but sanctify Christ as Lord in your heart, always being ready to make a defense to everyone who asks you to give an account for the hope that is in you, yet with gentleness and reverence; and keep a good conscience so that in the thing in which you are slandered, those who revile your good behavior in Christ will be put to shame. For it is better, if God should will it so, that you suffer for

doing what is right rather than doing what is wrong (1 Peter 3:13-17).

- She will overcome evil with good.

  Do not be overcome by evil, but overcome evil with good (Romans 12:21).

In addition to praying for your counselee, express love and kindness. Help her see that her household needs are met such as moving furniture, fixing a broken toilet, or cleaning the house if she is overwhelmed. These chores may not be your own personal responsibility but encourage her to ask her church for help.

Through love serve one another (Galatians 5:13).

So then, while we have opportunity, let us do good to all people, and especially to those who are of the household of the faith (Galatians 6:10).

See also 1 Thessalonians 5:14-15 and 1 John 3:17.

As counselors, we are to demonstrate God's love, and therefore be compassionate (Deuteronomy 4:31, Psalm 72:13). Simple statements like, "I am so sorry that this has happened" are comforting to your counselee. We are to **"put on a heart of compassion"** (Colossians 3:12). We are also to be like our Lord Jesus as He was going through the villages and ministering to the people. **"Seeing the people, He felt compassion for them, because they were distressed and dispirited like sheep without a shepherd"** (Matthew 9:36).

Call her on occasion to check up on her as **"a friend loves at all times"** (Proverbs 17:17). Normally, I give my cell number to a counselee going through a divorce. It will be a judgment call on your part, but I have found that women do not take advantage of having that information, but only use it when absolutely necessary. I do, however, ask them not to put it on social media!

Speak the truth to her but do it very gently as **"love is kind,"** and we are to speak the truth in love (1 Corinthians 13:4; Ephesians 4:15). Remind her of the great hope that we have in our Lord. Also, remind her often of the goodness of God and give her Scriptures to look up if she is upset. Read Psalm 37 and Psalm 42 to her. (Psalm 37 is the **"fret not because of evil doers"** Psalm. It will help her put the evil her husband is doing into an eternal perspective.)

Have her memorize Lamentations 3:21-25 so that she can be like Jeremiah remembering the hope she has in God.

> **This I recall to mind, therefore I have hope. The LORD's lovingkindnesses indeed never cease, for His compassions never fail. They are new every morning; great is Your faithfulness. "The LORD is my portion," says my soul, "therefore I have hope in Him." The LORD is good to those who wait for Him, to the person who seeks Him** (Lamentations 3:21-25).

The wife's great hope is that she can go through the divorce and have as her motive the glory of God, not a motive of desperately trying to hang on to her husband. If she is honoring God and going through her ordeal with His grace, she will be suffering for the Lord's sake, but if she is bitter and lashing out and slandering her husband to everyone who will listen, her suffering will be compounded by her own sin. The Apostle Peter explained how she should be reacting to her **"fiery ordeal"** (1 Peter 4:12).

> **Beloved, do not be surprised at the fiery ordeal among you, which comes upon you for your testing, as though some strange thing were happening to you; but to the degree that you share the suffering of Christ, keep on rejoicing, so that also at the revelation of His glory you may rejoice with exultation. If you are reviled for the name of Christ, you are blessed, because the Spirit of glory and of God rests on you** (1 Peter 4:12-14).

Some women make an idol out of waiting for their husbands to repent.

Counseling Women Going Through a Divorce

This could go on for years and may never be resolved. I am certainly not recommending anyone rushing into a divorce, but after she has gotten the "beam out of her own eye" and the church has completed church discipline on her husband (if he is a member of the church), then the elders, as well as the wife, should pray in faith for wisdom about the timing of filing for divorce. In James 1:2-6, God promises wisdom to respond rightly to trials as joy. In Hebrews 13:17, she is told to **"obey your leaders [in the church] and submit to them, for they keep watch over your souls as those who will give an account."** In my experience, a husband will rarely file for divorce. They mostly push their wives to file even if they are living in adultery with another woman.

Teach your counselee how to pray and plead with God regarding her husband. Remind her of the story of the unjust judge in Luke 18 and **"… will not God bring about justice for His elect who cry to Him day and night, and will He delay long over them?"** (Luke 18:7). Prepare her that one of two things is going to happen as she prays, and their church puts pressure on her husband to repent. Either his heart will soften, he will become humble and experience remorse over his sin, and thus God will grant him repentance, *or* God will turn him over to his depravity and give her a way of escape—divorce. In Romans 9:18 Paul wrote, **"So then He has mercy on whom He desires, and He hardens whom He desires."**

Scriptural Ways a Wife may Pray to God Concerning her Husband.
(All of these are based on what is best for God's reputation and glory. John 14:13; Psalm 106:7-8; Isaiah. 48:9-11; Psalm25:11; Romans 9)
1. God would soften his heart and grant him repentance. (2 Timothy 2:24-26)
2.The husband will not break the marriage vow that he made before God. (Matthew 19:1-9)
3. He will put God and others ahead of his own feelings and desires. (Matthew 22:36-40; 1 Corinthians13:4-7)

4. He will love his wife as Christ loved the church. (Ephesians 5:25-31)
5. He will delight in the law of the Lord and be blessed by God. (Psalm 1:1-3)
6. He will not be ungodly but will fear God. (Psalm 36:1:1)
7. He will hate evil. (Psalm 36:4)
8. He will not be like the man who lies in his bed and plots wickedness. (Psalm 36:3-4)
9. He will be "poor in spirit" and mourn over his sin. (Matthew 5:3-4)
10. He will be gentle and merciful. (Matthew 5:5-7)
11. He will hunger and thirst for righteousness. (Matthew 5:6)
12. He will stop manifesting the deeds of the flesh and start manifesting the fruit of the Spirit. (Galatians 5:19-23)
13. He will receive reproof and be clothed with humility. (1 Peter 5:5; Galatians 6:1; Matthew 18:15)
14. He will stop covering up his sin and find compassion instead. (Proverbs 28:13)
15. He will be like the prodigal son and return home. (Luke 15:11-32)
16. He will let the Word of Christ richly dwell within him. (Colossians 3:16)
17. He will not be double minded. (James 1:6-7)
18. He will turn away from evil. (Proverbs 3:7)

God will exert His Sovereign Will and she should pray with the attitude of "whatever would glorify God the most."

Early in the counseling process, help her get the beam out of her eye. That way she will be able to see clearly what her husband is doing. (See Matthew 7:1-6.) She will likely be struggling with fear, self-pity, bitter thoughts, and/or anger towards her husband and/or God. She will need to put off her anger and bitterness and replace it with kindness, a tender heart, and forgiveness. The basis of why she should forgive is **"just as God in Christ also has forgiven you"** (Ephesians 4:32). Do note that forgiving him does not mean that she should trust him. It would probably take a long while for him to re-earn her trust if he is even trying. Explain to her that forgiveness and trust are two separate issues.

Remind her that God is good and will reveal to her only what she can bear at that moment and no more. He will give her grace and strength as she needs it. God knows all that is happening, and He will **"deliver the needy when he cries for help"** (Psalm 72:12). One young woman I know told me that as she looked back on the confusion and unknowns while she was going through her divorce, she realized that God always prepared her for the next bit of distressing information that came to light. She viewed it as a kindness from God that He was good to her to let the bad news come out in stages and not all at once.

It is especially difficult for a wife when other people who love her and have taken up an offense for her have strong, dogmatic opinions about what she should do or not do. Some say, "You can never file; he has to file." "You can remarry, but only after the children are grown." "He has to marry first." "You have to wait two years or longer before you can remarry, and the clock starts ticking the day the divorce is final." Instead, her elders should be giving her guidance based on Scriptural principles. What really matters is biblical wisdom and her freedom in the Lord.

One day she might call you crying her heart out over what her lawyer has told her to expect. Examples are, "You will have to split the debt even though your husband incurred it all." "You won't be able to see your children on Christmas day except every other Christmas day." "You might as well get a job. Women don't get alimony anymore." Tell her these things may or may not happen. God is still in control and He *can* channel her husband's heart and the judge's heart. She can petition the court for what she wants, but if a judge orders differently then she must accept the ruling and comply and still give glory to God.

Often her husband makes threats and tries to bully her. He may hang up on her when he does not get his way or threaten, "I will take the children away from you" or "I'll never give you custody of the children" or "I'll take you to court and tell everyone what you did …" He may curse and scream at her. He is acting like a fool, and she should reply with something like, "If you do those things it will be difficult for me, but God will give me grace to bear up under it." (Proverbs 26:4-5; 1 Corinthians 10:13). Explain to her that if her husband is threatening or abusive with his language, she should quietly say, "I am not going to let you talk to me that way. If you do not calm down, I will just simply hang up." Then if she hangs up, just do it quietly—don't slam the phone down.

Help her to think rightly when she hears through the grapevine that her husband is making comments about her that are untrue or malicious. Another difficult scene for her is to hear about her husband and his girlfriend laughing and talking in a restaurant or strolling hand in hand through the mall or worse yet, they are doing that with the wife's children and the girlfriend's children. Remind her of what Peter wrote, **"Beloved, do not be surprised at the fiery ordeal among you, which comes upon you for your testing ..."** (1 Peter 4:12). This would probably be a good time to remind her of the **"Fret not..."** (Psalm 37).

Another likely outcome that will be very difficult for her is if her in-laws side with her husband and pull away from her and her family even when he is unrepentant and under church discipline. It is sad and dishonoring to God when parents will not back up the church with the discipline of their son. To me, it is scary for the in-laws as they will someday answer to God. Tell her you are sorry and what they are doing is not right. Pray for her and exhort her to be kind to her in-laws and give them blessings instead. (See Romans 12:21 and 1 Peter 3:8-9.)

How to Help Her Not be Consumed with Bitterness.

In emotionally charged situations such as separation and divorce, it is common for the wife to cultivate a root of bitterness in her heart which may even extend to family members who are inclined to take sides. Hebrews 12:15 says, **"See to it that no one fails to obtain the grace of God; that no root of bitterness springs up and causes trouble, and by it many become defiled."**

- Encourage her to remind herself of her sin against God and how much God has forgiven her. This will help her to be humble under God's hand and keep things in perspective. (See 1 Peter 5:6).
- She must remember that God is the defender of those suffering for righteousness sake. Romans 12:19 tells us to **"never take your own revenge, beloved, but leave room for the wrath of God, for it is written 'Vengeance is mine I will repay, says the Lord.'"**
- She must keep crying out to God for wisdom. He promises to give it to her. (See James 1:5-6).
- She is not to fret because of what her husband has done or is doing. (See Psalm 37).
- She should face the reality of the circumstances, but with a *great* reliance on God. Her earthly security may be gone but her heavenly Father will never leave, forsake, or disappoint her (Romans 10:11).
- She should think of her husband and what he is doing in biblical terms such as adulterer, scoffer, an unbeliever departing, homosexual, etc. and set her heart on giving God glory whether her husband repents or not. (See Psalm 1).
- She should treat her unrepentant husband (in a biblical sense) as her enemy. She should think of him not as an enemy she hates, but as an enemy she is to love (Romans 12:20-21). She should fight back with kind words overcoming evil, going the second mile (Matthew 7), turning the other cheek when appropriate (Matthew 7:39).
- She should remind herself that vengeance belongs to God and not her and if God never grants her husband repentance, the only happiness (and it is fleeting and probably not as wonderful as it may seem on the outside) her husband will ever have is right here and now (temporal). Soon, all the seeming happiness that he has will be gone and he will face the judgment of God. She is to do these things for God's glory and to try to help her husband but not as a manipulation tactic or magic formula (if I do this, then God will do that) to make the other person act right. If God is hardening his heart, the more godly she is, the meaner he will be because **"... everyone who does evil hates**

- **the Light"** (John 3:20). Overcoming evil glorifies God and protects her own heart from bitterness.
- If she has children, they need hope, a lot of hope. Counsel her to tell them the truth but not the sordid details. For example, "What Daddy is doing is wrong, but we need to pray for him and whether he repents or not, God will help us and we will be all right." She will be helping her children to face reality but with a hope in God (Philippians 4:8).

Conclusion

Going through a divorce is devastating and grievous, but it does not have to be in vain. Your counselee does not have to and should not spend days, months, or years looking for what the world calls her "worth". She can from the outset of the trial go through the process with great grace from God, great hope, and great comfort. She not only can hold fast to the Lord through prayer and His Word, but she can also exhort and help others (including her children, parents, siblings, and friends) to forgive and overcome evil with good. She can, by God's grace, see His goodness throughout the process and be able to look back (when all is said and done) and see God's providential hand that was at work and thank Him for the trial.

Chapter Twelve

Counseling Women Who Struggle with Pornography

I heard about a pastor's wife who told a young woman seeking help for her pornography addiction, "That's ridiculous, only men are addicted to porn." Well, nothing could be further from the truth. Statistics are alarming about women's pornography use. It is a real and present danger and getting worse. Crystal Renaud of "Dirty Girl Ministries" writes that it is common for women to think, "I thought I was the only one." She also writes that "…unlike for men, the addiction to porn in women is not as much about how it makes her feel physically, but how it meets her emotional needs."[31]

In this day of cell phones, iPads, and computers, it is quite easy for a woman to become addicted to some sort of lust/romantic fantasy scenarios. Here is an example of a counselee's testimony. This involved a man she never met and only knew what he told her about himself:

> "It all started very innocently, playing a game on the computer. I initially played with a Christian family, my sister, and my sons. I had a character who interacted with others from all over the country. I made online friends with several people and one person in particular. We had been friends for over a year and then our conversations started turning more personal. He was a married man, not happily married. His wife had cheated on him, so this seemed to be his justified outlet. Little by little our conversations became more intimate. We progressed from chat during the game to email and cell phone interactions. I liked having someone to share personal stuff with and it did not feel as wrong as it would have been if we were in person. Since he was in New York and it was just the internet, it was easier to make excuses. I really struggled with what I was doing. I knew it was wrong, but I could not seem to say no, or at least turn him away. We engaged in sexual talk

---

[31] Renaud, Crystal. *Dirty Girls Come Clean* (Chicago, IL: Moody Publishers, 2011), p.26.

and texting and I was addicted. Finally, I confessed my sin to my sister and Martha Peace so that I would have someone other than myself to hold me accountable. I slowed down until I finally made the break completely and deleted all available resources. The Lord has been gracious to forgive me and to remove the desire from me. With time, it has gotten easier and thankfully I do not wish to try to contact him."

Struggles like this often start off innocently, clicking the wrong button on the computer or viewing pornography at her husband's request or reading a romance novel that has vivid, sensual scenes.

As counselors we should take a woman's plea for help seriously and take her through what I am calling "Four Phases of Biblical Counseling." During all the phases, as a counselor you hold your counselee accountable for her actions. Let's begin with counseling phase one:

Phase One:
Teach Biblical Principles on Mortifying the Flesh

(The following principles were adapted from Arthur Pink's book, *The Doctrine of Mortification*)

To mortify the flesh means to discipline the natural desires and appetites of the physical body so that they are our servants and not our masters. In other words, we do not have to keep giving in to the sinful desires of our flesh. The Apostle Paul expressed it this way, **"...but I discipline my body and make it my slave..."** (1 Corinthians 9:27). It is a fact that because of Christ's resurrection from the dead, we *can* **"walk in newness of life ... our body of sin is done away with, so that we would no longer be slaves to sin..."** (Romans 6:4-7).[32]

Unmortified sin is against the whole design of the Gospel. It is as though Christ's sacrifice was intended to make us free *to* sin rather

---

[32] Pink, Arthur. *The Doctrine of Mortification.* (Pensacola, FL: Free Grace Broadcaster, Issue 201), p. 2.

than redeem us *from* it. Paul acknowledges that our freedom means that we do not have to keep sinning. We are a slave to righteousness **"having been freed from sin …"** we are now free to *not* sin (Romans 6:18-20).

Until a believer goes to be with the Lord in heaven, there is a ceaseless conflict between their *indwelling* sin and *God's* grace. Believers are indwelt with the Holy Spirit who convicts us of our sin, so the conflict continues while we are here on earth. **"For the flesh sets its desire against the Spirit, and the Spirit against the flesh; for these are in opposition to one another, so that you may not do the things that you please"** (Galatians 5:17).[33]

Even though our position in union with Christ is secure for all of eternity, we are nevertheless not to give in to our fleshly desires. We do that by setting our minds **"… on the things above, not on the things that are on earth."** We are to **"… consider the members of your earthly body as dead to immorality, impurity, passion, evil desires, and greed…"** (Colossians 3:1-5).[34]

The astounding good news for the Christian is that we no longer *have* to sin. God gives us a new nature, strengthens us in the inner man, grants fresh supplies of grace from day to day, works in us a loathing of sin, a mourning over it, a turning from it, presses the claims of Christ to us, brings up some biblical principles or warning to our mind, seals promises upon our hearts, and moves us to pray.[35]

> **So then, brethren, we are under obligation, not to the flesh, to live according to the flesh – for if you are living according to the flesh, you must die; but if by the Spirit you are putting to death the deeds of the body, you will live. For all who are being led by the Spirit of God, these are sons of God** (Romans 8:12-14).

Explain to your counselee that she is to be *active* in the work of mortifying her sin. It must not be supposed that the Holy Spirit will help

---

[33] Ibid, p 3.

[34] Ibid, p 2

[35] Ibid, p.3.

us without our cooperation. Believers are required to set themselves seriously to the task. Let not the lazy Christian imagine he will ever get the victory over his lusts as we are to **"discipline ourselves for the purpose of godliness"** (1 Timothy 4:7). We are to **"cleanse ourselves from all defilement of flesh and spirit, perfecting holiness in the fear of God"** (2 Corinthians 7:1).

So, she is to work at this, but the success and glory belong to God. He illumines her understanding and makes her more conscious of her sin. He deepens her yearnings after purity. He makes her conscience more sensitive. Our responsibility is to heed His convictions, to respond to His holy impulses, to implore His aid, to count upon His grace.[36]

> **So then, my beloved, just as you have always obeyed, not as in my presence [Paul's] only, but now much more in my absence, work out your salvation with fear and trembling, for it is God who is at work in you, both to will and to work for His good pleasure** (Philippians 2:12-13, explanation mine).

Phase Two:
Repentance Results in Confession and Accountability

I love a quite simple sentence that Jay Adams tells his counselees: "God is in the problem." There is nothing that the counselee has done that God cannot forgive or help them overcome. Sin is common to man; therefore, she is not the only one (1 Corinthians 10:13). Tell her that the Lord will help her, and you will help her. She needs to **"draw near with confidence to the throne of grace, so that** [she] **may receive mercy and find grace to help in time of need"** (Hebrews 4:16, explanation mine). Your responsibility as her counselor is to **"admonish the unruly, encourage the fainthearted, help the weak, be patient with everyone"** (1 Thessalonians 5:14, see also Galatians 6:2).

It is also helpful for your counselee to be told that what she has done by seeking counsel is wise (Proverbs 12:15). Do not promise to keep what she tells you a secret. Normally you would, but if it becomes an

---
[36] Ibid, p.5-6.

unrepentant church discipline matter, then you would have to bring in other witness. As a strict rule, I do not even tell my husband or the elders in my church what counselees tell me. To do otherwise, would simply be gossiping. The exception would be if the counselee is not doing well, such as being unrepentant or unstable emotionally. I will tell the elder in charge of our counseling ministry. Another exception would be if she is suicidal, then her family needs to know and take appropriate action.

Exhort your counselee to repent. Repentance is a turning from sin and a willingness to do whatever it takes to change. She should confess her sin to God and to the people she knows she has personally sinned against because of it. God promises that **"if we confess our sins, He is faithful and righteous to forgive us our sins and to cleanse us from all unrighteousness"** (1 John 1:9). The Lord Jesus instructs us that if we know someone has something against us, we are to make it a priority to go and confess our sin to that brother. (See Matthew 5:23-24.)

If your counselee is married, she should tell her husband, but not tell the sordid details. For example, "I have been secretly looking at internet pornography and masturbating for the last four years. I have sinned against God and you. I have asked God to forgive me and now I am asking you to forgive me." It is particularly important to prepare her for what her husband *might* say. If he says, "I forgive you," then she should simply say, "Thank you." If he says, "I do not forgive you," then she should say, "I don't blame you, but if you ever decide that you will, please tell me." If he says, "Well, that is in the past, so we won't talk about it now." Then she should take that as a "no" answer. He may not be meaning "no", but it is awkward for him and he does not know quite what to say. So, she should say, "I don't blame you for not saying, 'I forgive you,' but if you come to the place where you can say it, please let me know."

If your counselee is opposed to confessing to her husband, then I think Heath Lambert's book, *Finally Free*,[37] would help persuade her of the need for a clear conscience. There may be a good reason she does not want to confess to her husband, such as her husband having a violent

---

[37] Lambert, Heath, *Finally Free*, (Grand Rapids, MI, Zondervan, 2013)

temper, so listen to her explanation and pray together for wisdom. After she confesses to God and to her husband, her main accountability partner needs to be someone other than her husband; someone who is comfortable to listen to the truth and support her with prayer.

Phase two also includes making no provision for her flesh. That includes her smart phone, computer, I Pad, romance books (even Christian romance books), severing any associated internet or face-to-face relationships and blocking numbers. Someone else should have her password to her computer for probably a year or two, and/or someone to be nearby when she is on the computer. Other provisions for the flesh could be certain music or alcohol. If she is repentant, accountability will be a joy and a relief to her that she is finally safe from easy exposure.

Phase Three:
What to do with Pornographic/Romance Images that Come to Mind

Favorite images or romantic scenarios will come to mind often, so instruct her to pray and beg God to erase the image. Exhort her to ask God that she would forget to the point where she would not even be able to recall them. At first, she possibly could be confessing this sin and praying fifty times a day.

Help her have a "trigger-quick" response to the first scenes that flood into her mind. A few years ago, I saw a You Tube video of a robbery in progress in a liquor store. The owner was behind the cash register and the security video camera was on the wall up over his shoulder. A very innocent looking middle-aged man walked up and drew a gun on the owner. The owner instantly did two things at once – took his left hand and pushed the robber's gun to the side and drew his own gun. It was unexpected and I cheered. When I thought about it later, that owner must have practiced those simultaneous moves hundreds of times. Likewise, we are to help our counselee have emergency pure thoughts so that when the sinful thought pops up in her brain, she will have so disciplined herself for the purpose of godliness that she will have an immediate righteous "trigger" thought that is pure. Help her come up with pure, God-honoring thoughts based on Romans 12:1-2, Ephesians 4:22-24, and Philippians 4:8.

Give her homework to memorize pure thoughts and be able to say them easily out loud to you the next week. Here are some examples:

PURE, GOD-HONORING THOUGHTS
"Lord, I am coming boldly to Your throne of grace because I need *Your* mercy and grace to help me *not* to sin against You." (Hebrews 4:16)
"Lord I know that You called me not in impurity but in holiness. Make me pure in my heart so that I might not sin against You." (1 Thessalonians 4:7)
"Forgive me for this thought I just had. I know that since I asked You, You *are* faithful and just to forgive me and cleanse me from all unrighteousness" (1 John 1:9).
"Lord, I want to set my mind on You and the things above, not on this earth. I am asking You to renew my mind so much that I cannot even remember my sinful thought." (Colossians 3:2)
"Lord, may Your love constrain me." (2 Corinthians 5:14)
"Thank You *so much* for helping me." (1 Thessalonians 5:18)
"Bless the Lord, O my soul. O LORD my God, *You* are very great!" (Psalm 104:1-2)

Phase Four:
Dying to Self and Becoming Consumed with the Glory of God

Sinful people are "at heart" pleasure seekers, and her only sin is not going to be pornography or illicit online or in person sexual relationships. Her pornography/romance addiction temporarily relieves boredom, anxiety, romance fantasies, or intimacy desires. She must now seek her pleasure from God. I suggest writing out a prayer for her to pray in her own words but here is the idea:

Prayer Asking to be Consumed with the Glory of God
"Lord I want so badly to please You. Help me have control over my body, not in the passion of lust, but in holiness and honor to You." (1 Thessalonians 4:5)
"Lord, help me to be consumed with Your glory in every area of my life – ministry to my husband, kids, money, whatever I eat and drink – all for Your glory." (1 Corinthians 10:31)
"Renew my mind that I will be focused on the things above, not on this earth." (Colossians 3:2)
"Use me for Your glory no matter what that means." (John 14:13)

To help her become more enamored of God have her read and study through Arthur Pink's book, *The Attributes of God* or Martha Peace's book, *Precious Truths in Practice*. I do not recommend resources that are man-centered, seeking to have your need for significance, worth, or even your identity needs presented in a "man-centered" way. Also avoid any twelve step programs, group therapy, or books that give examples of sordid details. Instead, I highly recommend Heath Lambert's book *Finally Free*. Either teach her or take her through *Attitudes of a Transformed Heart* by Martha Peace chapter nine which is "How to Think Biblically." One more resource that would be helpful to teach her a pure perspective on sexual intimacy between husband and wife is *The Excellent Wife* by Martha Peace.

Conclusion

Pornography/ romance addiction in women is on the rise and is a tightly guarded secret. It is either adultery or fornication in her heart. Counselors should not be shocked as this is a sin that is common to man. Instead, we should make it as easy as possible for others to approach us if they are seeking help!